T0332264

ORPHEUS IN THE UNDERWORLD

THE GERMAN LIST

THEODOR W. ADORNO

Orpheus in the Underworld

Essays on Music and Its Mediation

TRANSLATED BY DOUGLAS ROBERTSON

LONDON NEW YORK CALCUTTA

This publication has been supported by a
grant from the Goethe-Institut India.

Seagull Books, 2024

The source texts of this translation can be found in volumes 17, 18, 19 and 20
of Theodor W. Adorno's *Gesammelte Schriften in 20 Bänden*.

© Suhrkamp Verlag, Frankfurt am Main, 1982–86

First published in English translation by Seagull Books, 2024
English translation © Douglas Robertson, 2024

ISBN 978 1 80309 322 2

British Library Cataloguing-in-Publication Data
A catalogue record for this book is available from the British Library

Typeset by Seagull Books, Calcutta, India
Printed and bound in the USA by IBI

CONTENTS

Translator's Note

When referring to a musical composition, Adorno often does not provide its full title or the title by which it is now best known, as is understandable in a series of essays written when most of the works discussed in them were new. I have done my best to preserve this stylistic quality while providing clarifications where necessary. To merely incomplete titles, I have supplied the missing part in square brackets. English translations of German titles are also presented in square brackets. Where more clarification is needed, I have supplied it (generally the minimum amount needed to distinguish the work from others by the same composer or with an identical or near-identical title) in a footnote to the chronologically earliest occurrence of the potentially unclear reference. I have treated names of persons similarly—footnoting them only when the first name is omitted and the person is not a well-known figure in music history; thus, 'Scott' and 'Egk' are footnoted but 'Delius' and 'Hermann Prey' are not.

BÉLA BARTÓK

So far, our acquaintance with the corpus of this Hungarian who has just reached the zenith of his artistic power is quite fragmentary. His works are only sporadically performed here; recently, his name has at least been appearing more frequently on the recital-programs of pianists. There is not much by him that is even accessible in the form of published scores. It is therefore difficult to say anything about him, and a caveat must be appended to a fair amount of what can be said. But he undoubtedly figures among the essential musicians of the present day.

His native country brims over with music, the music of wanderers, of the hot-blooded, of the homeless who are nevertheless perfectly at home there—but also with the music of the dull-witted, of those who are bound to the earth, of people whose very blood has been settled by the country's infinite low-slung horizons and whose pulse is measured out by their rhythms. Magyars and Gypsies clash with each other in its sound, which ebbs and flows abruptly and sluggishly, wearily and youthfully, in song and on horseback. The music of the great Pan retains its abode here; from the shaggy sensuality of its faun's lyre, the dread of being walked in on by a

---

'Béla Bartók' (1922) in Theodor W. Adorno, *Gesammelte Schriften in 20 Bänden* (Rolf Tiedemann, Gretel Adorno, Susan Buck-Morss and Klaus Schultz eds) (Frankfurt am Main: Suhrkamp, 2017), 'Band 18: Musikalische Schriften V'.

third party still erupts at point-blank range and in copious quantities. Here music still stirs in the very soul of the nation; here it retains its epic timelessness, which forgoes the ego discharged from the community of nature and borne along by both time and a singularly peculiar destiny. Here, when an individual becomes a bearer of music, he does not become a self of spontaneous creativity and sequestered responsibility but rather a national hero, a person who representatively epitomizes his entire nation without becoming problematic in their eyes, a man plain and simple in the Roman sense, an embodiment of *virtus*. And so Hungarian musicians become 'virtuosos', guys who tame the piano or the violin even better— albeit no differently—than their confreres. Modern Europe—Vienna and Germany and Paris—is barging into this world; a barbaric civilization is opening up to the outside world and spasmodically refashioning its peculiar naivety into transgression. A thin layer is bravely and tenaciously detaching itself from the remainder, taking the curse of individuation onto its sturdy shoulders and devoting its colossal innate energies—the energies of the individual (which does not yet merely signify the individual here!)—to completing the circle delimiting a home-grown culture. Here perchance is the historical setting in which we must quest for Béla Bartók.

His beginnings were not radically different from those of the typical well-trained musician of the periphery of the Wagner school at the turn of the century. His Rhapsody for Piano and Orchestra, op. 1 [Sz. 27],[1] is a thematically fresh, consistently homophonic piece that is strikingly virtuosic and a world away from problematic

---

1 Owing to Bartók's irregular assignment of opus numbers to his compositions, all references to these works in this volume are followed by the numbers assigned to them by András Szőllősy and prefaced by 'Sz.' [Trans.]

contents and technical complexity. The Suite [No. 1] for full orchestra, op. 3 [Sz. 31], which Eugen Szenkar introduced to German concertgoers in Frankfurt last season, alludes to the polyphony of *Die Meistersinger*. It brings to bear a naively pictorial impressionism of natural landscapes with great aural charm without uninterruptedly coming to terms with a malleable formal goal. In both works, one encounters a 'national' element in the form of Gypsy-style voice-leading and syncopated formulas, an element which for all its prevalence contributes no more to the overall structure than, say, the Russian colour scheme that Tchaikovsky delighted in sporting at the cosmopolitan fancy-dress ball of civilization going primitive. In the Suite No. 2 (op. 4 [Sz. 34], for small orchestra), a playful spirit reigns supreme within scantier dimensions. A break was subsequently bound to ensue. The fourteen piano pieces, op. 6 [Sz. 38], styled 'Bagatelles' with coquettish coyness, show a completely altered face. It is not the fact that he has adopted Debussy's method and is now subverting tonality via recourse to the whole-tone scale, and occasionally even to the old church modes, that gives these pieces their distinctive stamp. They are agglomerated with astonishing concentration; the question of the necessity of every beat is tackled head-on and often compresses entire emotive arcs within the confines of a taut, perfervid rhythmic complex. Paris is certainly not treated with kid gloves: 'Elle est morte' [No. XIII] moans half-ironically, and 'Ma mie qui danse' [No. XIV] shines like a concave mirror pilfered from Montmartre. But a storm that does not sit well on the Mediterranean azure of Debussy's cove is already brewing here, and the tenth piece is already a proper Allegro barbaro.[2] What he had to

---

2 In other words, despite being marked merely Allegro, the tenth bagatelle in its fury and technique anticipates Bartók's freestanding short piano work, *Allegro*

say could not be said in French, and this dawned on him here at his turning-point: he therefore then made a clean break with all the salon-music-peddling Slavs of his time and unsheathed his nationalism, which he employed as a rough-and-ready corrective to his nervous sensibility. He worked assiduously as a collector, travelling from village to village, transcribing Magyar and Rumanian folksongs as the brothers Grimm had transcribed their fairy tales and collaborating with Zoltán Kodály on a scholarly account of his activities. Living music owes to this period his piano arrangements of peasant songs and peasant dances along with children's pieces and a 'Sonatina' [Sz. 55] based on national melodies that richly mines the vein of the old modes and bears favourable comparison to Brahms' arrangements of folksongs. But he never succumbed to the allure of a 'retrograde utopia'; he never turned naive and leapt back into the good old days. In contrast to Schoenberg's atonality, his system of harmony is dominated by a brusque delight in dissonance in which consonance is still secretly, tacitly kept in mind all the while. He is turning to the composition of chamber music, and without abandoning the differentiation of modern sonata form, he is strengthening its backbone via his firm, capacious system of rhythm, in which his soul encounters that of his people. The traditional schema is completely absorbed into this system; the boisterous vigour of the movements arches over the duality of the themes, which only flare up like campfires during a horseback ride through the steppes. In technical terms, his two string quartets (opp. 7 [Sz. 40] and 17 [Sz. 67]), to whose style that of the new Violin Sonata, op. 21 [No. 1, Sz. 75], would seem to be affined, constitute a *critique of sonata form*. Each of them confines itself to a count of

---

barbaro [Sz. 49], which he composed in 1911, five years after the *14 Bagatelles*. [Trans.]

three movements; scherzo, rondo and allegro-like sections converge with one another; the adagio tempo rhapsodically acts overwrought and points into the dusky distance. In the Second Quartet, this structural principle is brought into sharp focus. Its first movement exhibits a motivically anchored sonata form with two overlapping thematic groups, a development and a recapitulation; its second, quite rhythmically conservative and homophonic in texture, is a scherzo in spirit but closer to a rondo in structure; it disembogues into a hard-driven stretto whose al-fresco bearing is entirely new to chamber music. The adagio is placed at the end. By comparison with this tightly caulked work, the First Quartet comes across as the product of improvisation; it abruptly juxtaposes extremes like a Gypsy's fiddle. Its expansively lyrical introduction is especially heartfelt. Bartók's piano works, which become increasingly ruthless up to the uncommonly difficult Studies, op. 18 [Sz. 72], have remained more narrowly subjective than the quartets: in them the virtuoso lets off steam. The comparatively simple Suite, op. 14 [Sz. 62], may be recommended as an introduction to them.

In addition to several orchestral works (opp. 5, 10 and 12),[3] Bartók has written two works for the stage whose performance at the Frankfurt Opera is in the offing: *Bluebeard's Castle*, op. 11 [Sz. 48], and *The Wooden Prince*, op. 13 [Sz. 60], a pantomime. Their libretti were written by Béla Balász. Bartók's inner essence is becoming manifest. In Bartók's instrumental compositions, terror appears from out of nowhere and smashes to pieces the security of the merely performative with dull hammer-blows, and his music is extremely unsettling in every respect; consequently, the opera *Bluebeard's Castle* is instinct with menace. The irruption of the

---

3 Op. 5: Two Portraits for Violin and Orchestra, Sz. 37; op. 10: Two Pictures, Sz. 46; op. 12: Four Pieces, Sz. 51. [Trans.]

eternalism of nature into the human world is its eternal theme, a theme into which, doubtless unbeknownst to himself, his conception of the mentality of his people has hardened. In contrast to civilized poets, he has no need of half-symbols and ambiguous symbols; the image and its meaning alike collapse under the primitiveness of his artistic gaze. *Bluebeard*'s libretto is basically a horror movie-esque reworking of *Lohengrin*'s, but Bartók unceremoniously dispenses with all stage magic and elicits from the script a profundity that was certainly not intended by its author. The plot device of seven doors in a row opening in alternating mood-lighting affords him his structural schema of seven self-contained movements, the first and last of which alone share thematic material. But these movements are like variations on the theme lying behind the music—the theme of terror, a terror that ascends, blazes forth from a dazzling major-mode refulgence, undulates in turbid billows, savagely rears up to its full height and seeps away into the night in the conclusion, which dissolves into the silence of the beginning at an adagio pace. An acerbically simple orchestral frame has been stretched around these emotional proceedings. In much the same way in which *Bluebeard* concentrates Bartók's underlying tragic powers, *The Wooden Prince*, a ballet with an agreeably innocuous scenario, gathers together his sublunarily vectored rhythmic riches, pours them into an iridescent orchestra and floods the world with dance. But this dance is warmer than Stravinsky's: it is not a romantic version of the grotesque; rather, it is a dance that, amid the most finely honed craftsmanship, beams itself directly and unreservedly at us from the primal emotions of love, defiance, sorrow and happiness.

1922

6

It may not be amiss to make a few remarks regarding Bartók's recently premiered work, which was the most resoundingly successful item on the program of the Prague Music Festival apart from Alban Berg's Fragments from *Wozzeck*.

The piece is not termed a suite out of modesty or coquettishness; it is most certainly not a symphony, and it does not aspire to seem symphonic in a single one of its loosely shaped measures. It owes its existence to a chance occasion; it was composed for a concert celebrating the fiftieth anniversary of the unification of Buda and Pest and is therefore an occasional work even in spirit. One will search it in vain for the tempestuousness and tranquillity of the great First Violin Sonata, for the adventures in sonority, rhythm and form that took place in the Second [Sz. 76]. A handful of transparent, catchy dance tunes are loosely concatenated; the ritornellos that bind them together merely fill out rests instead of attempting to organize the work as a whole in some fashion; and even the finale, which contains references to the thematic material of the earlier movements, juxtaposes this familiar material with watertight innocuousness and without even going through the motions of

---

'Béla Bartók Tanzsuite' (1925) in *Gesammelte Schriften*, 'Band 18: Musikalische Schriften V'.

attempting a synthesis, without even bothering to introduce much in the way of contrapuntal overlapping. Essentially simpler in harmonic terms than one has come to expect of Bartók, the suite is founded on a thinly veiled diatonicism intermittently perforated by enharmonic fourths, a harmonic foundation rather like that of the Piano Suite, op. 14 [Sz. 62]. It is winsomely and elegantly orchestrated in accordance with its raison d'être. It also comports itself with simplicity in the organization of its individual movements; the thematic groups are expounded, then often repeated several times in immediate succession in and at various registers and dynamic levels; new material follows, and the beginning returns, sometimes in its unaltered entirety, sometimes in the form of a succinct quotation; there are no development sections. The Adagietto (the fourth movement)[1] is a kind of primitive dialogue; recumbent string chords chock-full of mellow arpeggiated seconds alternate in unruffled equability with unison phrases from solo woodwinds. Only the third dance and the finale are divided into multiple sections. In short, the suite is guileless in intention and glibly unpretentious in execution. For all that, it is significantly characteristic not only of the composer himself, who remains true to himself as always in it, but also of the general situation from which it originates.

What is one actually to make of the fact that an audaciously personal and tenaciously radical artist like Bartók has accepted a commission to write an occasional work and then adhered to the specifications of that commission in the course of writing it? One would have expected this man, whose critique of the traditional

---

1 The fourth movement of the *Dance Suite* is actually marked Molto tranquillo. [Trans.]

sonata once extended to the rhapsodic dissolution of all prescribed form, to be fashioning forms of his own in unfettered liberty now; heretofore he consistently forged his own path to a realm where his subjective plenitude still harmonized with the tried-and-true existence of musical stereotypes, an existence that certainly narrows a nation's options but by the same token affords it a substantial guarantee of authenticity—and could he now actually be circumspectly surveying his surroundings and retracing his steps back to territories in which that stereotyping is valid yet makes no provision for the ego? Indeed, he is turning back occasionally, and in a well-founded manner. His relationship to Hungarian folk music, to rhapsody, monody and dance, is not as secure as espousers of the creed of Romanticism fondly wish for it to be. The fault line that causes the ego and form to go their separate ways even in Bartók's work is too deep, the space in which they arduously make peace with each other is too confined, the path that leads to that space is simply too narrow, not to take one's breath away. However deeply Bartók may lean into isolated subjectivism (his work even contains passages that might almost have been written by Webern!), the dialectic of his position may still require him to engage with forms that give no quarter to him as a person, that strangely cut against the grain of his essential character and at the same time temptingly appeal to him and thereby prevent him from completely sinking away into himself.

As Bartók responds to this temptation without succumbing to it in the *Dance Suite*, his strength holds its own under the veil of a guileless incipience.

He knows—not in conscious reflection, to be sure, but in his capacity as a fashioner of art—that the forms that have torn themselves free of the ego and rigidified in their isolation have lost their binding power over the ego, that every trace of intrinsic reality has evaporated from them; and he refrains from employing them as if they were real. But he also knows that the forms are still here even if they no longer exist, that their demands still incessantly impinge on the ego even if it is no longer adequate to them just as they are no longer adequate to it. The zone of reconciliation that remains left to him is affording him no reposeful sojourn; he cannot help incessantly striving to force open each side of it. If he is passing over into the sphere of pure subjectivism, at the same time he is being fortified by his national affiliation; if he is setting foot in the sphere of dead forms, at the same time he is being kept alive by his ego. Instead of pathetically struggling with the reality of the forms or romantically simulating them, he *plays* with them, lets them be summoned by the occasion, which becomes a symbol of contingency, the contingency that has become the sole governor of the relation to such forms; he does not attempt to encumber and perforate them with subjectivity; rather, he bares his soul precisely in the worldly-wise irony with which he keeps his secret. And again, he is kept on his feet by the folksy ground beneath them; the alienation of his person from the forms is not complete; he retains some stock in them and they in him; his play does not turn into playfulness.

In Bartók's *Dance Suite*, the problem of music as play becomes paradigmatically clear and its profound contemporary relevance comes to light; it is a problem harboured by Stravinsky's intention on a different level and in a darker sense. Stravinsky's music is becoming quite similar to that of this suite, although it must be conceded that Bartók can justly claim to have arrived at his own emancipation of rhythm, abrupt changes of metre and predilection for five-part structures in complete independence of the Russian. His *Dance Suite* will present no terrors to conductors who are managing to master the difficulties of *The Rite of Spring*, and even orchestras that are unaccustomed to virtuoso tasks of that kind will be able to cope with the piece. The peculiarity of its formal structure may ultimately secure him broad public acclaim even though it is very much a work of the present moment.

1925

REMARKS ON A FEW OF BÉLA BARTÓK'S WORKS

It is not the expansive scope of a talent broadly based in sensuousness that repeatedly compels one to grapple with Béla Bartók's mode of composition. Being a member of the same generation as Schoenberg and Stravinsky, and having grown out of the same general musical situation as that of their youth, in the course of his productive activity he found himself faced with the same problems as the ones that agitated each of them: he was also prompted by the question of how music was to grope its way home to the terra firma of complete reality from the crumbling terrain of a Romanticism permanently severed from human existence, or, should such terra firma prove unreachable, how music was to expose the latter's unreality in its perfective assertion of that unreality and polemically adumbrate a means of overcoming it. But whereas Schoenberg, blindly subservient to the question, raised the sheen of semblance to a liquescent incandescence, left nothing unattempted and above all allowed himself to succumb to every temptation in the attempt to encounter himself afterwards in the quickened plenitude of dynamic spiritual art; whereas Stravinsky in his outrageous self-assurance transparently made semblance into dialectical annihilation, laid bare its iron skeleton in order to make its glad rags billow out and ultimately built

'Über einige Werke von Béla Bartók' (1925) in *Gesammelte Schriften*, 'Band 18: Musikalische Schriften V'.

this iron skeleton into the world as the latter's house, in which it was expected to take up residence with a shiver; whereas both Schoenberg *and* Stravinsky traversed the chaos of the evanescent forms from end to end and hardened themselves against it, Bartók withdrew into himself as soon as the chaos began to impinge on him, and he searched for whatever traces of the real might still be left there or extracted from the forms, venturesomely braced for any danger the senses might throw his way there but simultaneously more sheltered and more impoverished than the adventurers into the realm of the soul. For his turn away from the dubious infinitude of psychologism resulted for him in the reduction of the musically actual to the dimensions of what in the way of existing forms was present in the *people*, in his people, in the music of Hungarian and Rumanian peasants; his soul lacks the audacity to roam beyond the confines of the community from which it has just received an affirmative reply. Bartók's confinement to himself is becoming necessary to his self-confinement; this self-confinement declines to engage in open combat with the problematic forms and excises from the ego the narrow region that has been relieved of the duty of attending to the problematic situation into which the surviving tried-and-tested forms are falling. His apperception of the folksong decisively parts company with every kind of Romantic apperception; it supplies the ego with correctives rather than with supplements; it critiques the ego's demand for musical autonomy; it emanates not from any fixed ideal of the folksong that might be striven after but rather from the real and extremely paradoxical scraps of singing that the collector puts on record and that he does not attempt to imitate but rather employs as a circumscriptive boundary to his own incipience; the veracity of this apperception becomes manifest in the

13

fact that in Bartók's works the vein of folk music is never discretely sequestered as an element of style but rather consistently comprehended and permeated by the entire subjective process of composition after the manner in which the ego and the objective realm permeate each other exclusively in the realm of the real.

But the homogeneity of form and ego, Bartók's blessing and limitation, requires his range of available formal types to be as restricted as his own psyche. There are only three such schemas that he strives to employ; folk music has peremptorily determined that these must be rhapsody punctuated by declamation, lyrically open-ended monody and passionately agitated dance; he received them as critiques of the essential instrumental forms—the sonata, the adagio and the scherzo or rondo; in his work, these last two concurrently recede to their origins. Bartók's riches are exhausted in his radical implementation of his critique, in his unalloyed delineation of types; he has really only written three pieces so far, and his development is nothing but the journey from the hidden kernel to the lucid visibility of these pieces. The journey was long and not without peril; Bartók willingly allowed himself to be seduced by musical impressionism, which he admittedly simplified so grossly for his own ends, which he understood in such crudely pictorial terms, that he scarcely managed to fashion his own musical manner in a serious sense. But he was deep enough to put up with aberrations that were capable of at least shaking if not quite shattering his sense of security, and there is no shortage of faux pas. It was only in the tightly wrought Piano Suite, op. 14, and the *Allegro barbaro* (also for piano) that he finally broke through into his focal point; in the expansively beautiful and completely unique [Second String] Quartet, op. 17, and in the Studies, op. 18, he took the next logical steps; now, in the two violin sonatas (UE 7247 and 7257),[1] his latest works of chamber music, he seems to have reached his goal.

Like the Second Quartet, the First Sonata is in three movements: these three movements perfectly exemplify Bartók's three pieces. The first movement, rhapsodically relaxed, has a sonata-form structure; its argument is expounded with watertight strictness, but it is quite free at the level of metre and melody; the second principal idea of the first group is fused with the bridge passage; the second group is again formed from two ideas, one with a halting gait and strong Hungarian coloration, and another that is boisterously propulsive and that leads in a swift intensification to the brief concluding group, which dies away into complete silence. The development ensues three times: first of all, the first idea of the second theme is nebulously, dulcimeresquely fetched forth as if from a great distance; then the principal theme begins adagio; finally, a reminiscence of the bridge passage inaugurates the lively third development section, whose motivic material hails from the first group. A curtailed recapitulation presents the themes in their original order and yet completely transformed. The exceedingly clear disposition of the movement holds its ground against all rhapsodic unruliness without hardening into rigidity and supports the heavy burden of mighty affects in the presence of whose awesome power all talk of national authenticity pales into literary prattle. The second movement (marked Adagio) avows its monadic origins even in its instrumentation: the unaccompanied violin executes a long-spun theme; this

---

1 These are the Universal Edition catalogue numbers of the scores of the two works. Adorno evidently inserts these numbers here because with the Violin Sonata No. 1, op. 21 (1921), Bartók stopped assigning opus numbers to his compositions. [Trans.]

alone should suffice to give the lie to the assertion that non-tonal music is melodically impotent; later the violin is joined by weirdly iridescent triads in the piano. Again the violin has the first word; again the piano undergirds its swansong chords. Above an iterated double-bass F-sharp on the piano that besieges the serried silence,[2] a middle episode rises up in abrupt accents; it subdivides into two sections; each section commences above a pedal point and is then spun out further by the piano on its own until the second one trickles away into mere noises. Then the violin returns with its song, now accompanied; soon it swirls its line around in varying directions in a Gypsy-like fashion; finally, it concentrates itself into a melos of the utmost intensity, a melos irradiated with harmonic warmth, and then peters out into the distant expanses whence it emerged. The third movement is both a rondo capriccioso and a stylized czardas; quite simple in design and with pronounced leanings towards C-sharp minor, it possesses great thematic pithiness and syncopal charm. The sonata makes extraordinary demands of both the piano and the violin and offers many spurs to virtuosos; it is rewarding in the maturity with which it shapes substantial content and takes unique advantage of this moment in which the reconciliation of musical internality and externality is possible. Once again a work that has bidden defiance to the sonata schema bids fair to have some staying power.

In the First Sonata, Bartók's critique had fallen silent in the presence of the rondo, which he accepted as it was, proclaiming what he had to say from within its frame, to be sure, but not fashioning its frame out of what he had to say. He began to fashion

---

2 The F-sharp two octaves below the bass clef. [Trans.]

such a frame in the Second Sonata. It consists of only two movements, which are thematically interconnected; the first is almost a kind of introduction, loosely tripartite, unrestrained; the second a dancelike piece, very extensive in its dimensions. This rondo is downright quodlibetesque in its unfetteredness; often one song-tune follows almost immediately on the heels of another, but its sustained urge to keep moving astonishingly keeps all particularity chained in place; its levitating architectonics is finely articulated thanks to repeated quotation of its central motif. Bartók courageously flirts with anarchism; he does not fight shy of fragments; he hones his sonority on jarring heaps of seconds until it attains a bizarre asperity, but the music keeps the work of composition going without requiring any intervention from him; every last vestige of bad conventionality has fallen away; he has become quite open about what he is doing. But at the same time, he has doubtless reached the limit of what must be achieved in his sphere.

For there undoubtedly is such a limit. The open-ended song has been termed his lyrical wellspring. Whenever he attempts to transition to self-contained Lied-like compositions, as in the five Ady Songs, op. 16 (published by Universal Edition),[3] and to add new formal types to his three original ones, he fails: he falls into a cheap psychologism that labels consonance good fortune and dissonance misfortune; he restricts his rich system of harmony to meeting the exigencies of a crude system of symbolism or even (as at one point in the first song) gets bogged down in stifling polytonality in the mould of Schrecker's, Scott's,[4] or Delius'. Even on a formal level

---

3 Five Songs on Poems by Endre Ady, Sz. 63 (1916). [Trans.]
4 Presumably the English composer Cyril Scott (1879–1970). [Trans.]

the songs are quite friable, and their accompaniment barely holds them together like so much musical sticky tape. His choice of text is certainly of dubious merit, even if the poems should turn out not to be as rebarbative in the original Hungarian as they are in the translator's travelling-salesmanesque German. The rhapsodizing vocal part yearns to function as the pith and marrow of the skeletonless voice leading but ends up simply swimming quite haphazardly above the piano part. But Bartók's total helplessness in a realm not marked out for him is rather an argument in his favour than in his disfavour. He hasn't a trace of savoir faire; he is completely subservient to the exigencies of his specific task; he is at home within himself, and when he stays at home, one must be grateful to him.

1925

The natural essence of music does not give rise to any timeless rules for indicating instructions to its performers. Like musical performance itself, these indications have their history—a history that reflects the varying tension between prescribed form and personal freedom. Today it may be assumed that we have reached a limit situation of a sort that has entailed the disappearance of this tension. Accordingly, it is perhaps needful to say the following:

The benefit of metronomization is that the composer's conception of a piece's tempo is rationally specified. As no objective formal tradition bindingly determines how a work is to be executed and, at the same time, works from this age do not allow the performer any degree of free play, such specification is necessary even though it admittedly could never assure the integrity of performances. The capriciousness of performers, which only asserts itself as the bad antithesis of playful performative freedom, is drastically forestalled by metronomization.

One must concede that metronomization contains a conceivable drawback in the very rational rigidity of its technical basis, which seems tailor-made to threaten that much-ballyhooed living life of a

---

'Metronomisierung' (1926) in *Gesammelte Schriften*, 'Band 17: Musikalische Schriften IV'.

performance. But in the first place, the application of the category of life to works of art—which are constructions, not creations—is dubious. Moreover, there are grounds for suspecting that this life is often no more than an ideology of the performers, who feel affronted by the demands of a self-contained work that exists even in the absence of their contribution and who attach more importance to their own laxity than to the life of the works, a life that admittedly does not take place between ritardando and a tempo but rather is to be found in the history of the works as interpreted in varying ways by performers, as is attested by Schoenberg's essay on mechanical musical instruments.[1] That a work cannot be performed strictly by the metronome—unless the work itself has mechanistic intentions—but that instead the metronome marking approximately supplies the modifiable basic unit of tempo, ought to go without saying and be unassailable by any pedantic doubts. Incidentally, Schoenberg has incisively circumscribed the ancillary function of the metronome markings in his 'George Lieder', op. 15.[2] The performer's liberal rule of thumb no longer suffices to define the interpretation; whereas, conversely, there is more room for better phrasing, better sound, a more faithful apprehension of the work at an adequate stage of its history—in other words, ultimately, more room for life—between three 'dead' but exact chronometric units than between private vacillations whose individualistic origin belongs

---

1 Arnold Schoenberg, 'Mechanische Musikinstrumente', *Pult und Taktstock* (March–April 1926): 71–75. Translated into English by Leo Black as 'Mechanical Musical Instruments' in *Style and Idea: Selected Writings of Arnold Schoenberg* (Berkeley: University of California Press, 1975), pp. 326–30. [Trans.]

2 *Das Buch der hängenden Gärten* [*The Book of the Hanging Gardens*], op. 15 (1909), a setting of 15 poems from Stefan George's collection of the same name. [Trans.]

to a stage of musical history that has had its day; a stage whose importunate vitality is in truth dead, a vitality manipulated according to set patterns.

The benefits outweigh the drawbacks; they outweigh them decisively and in praxis, which in this case cannot really be contrasted with theory, for the theory of musical performance alone specifies the latter's concrete requirements. Metronomization seems dubious to me only in the case of older works, which accord more to interpretative freedom; although the history of the metronomization of Bach in the nineteenth century, even if it is a history of errors, provides a worthy representation of the history of the works themselves. But because the decline of interpretative freedom is not only dictated by the structure of contemporary works but also conditioned by the remoteness from tradition of the performers' own situation, it is impossible to foresee whether the metronomization of works from other periods will soon also be necessary. The question whether, in progressing further in its phase of metronomization, older music is simultaneously entering a phase of mere preservation by antiquarians, whether its history is consequently drawing to a close, need not be discussed here. At the level of the particular, the beat will be obliged to gloss over many contradictions in the state of knowledge.

The composer may manage to obviate misunderstandings 'that can arise from the all-too-great precision of metronomization' via even greater precision—via, specifically, his introduction of several tempi (Tempo I, Tempo II, Tempo III, all metronomized) or his modification of the metronome count with every change in tempo indication, e.g.: Bewegt [active or animated] ($\quarternote = 120$) etwas ruhiger [somewhat calmer] ($\quarternote = 92$) straffer [tighter] ($\quarternote = 106$),

Hauptzeitmass [principal tempo] ($\downarrow$ = 120). Incidentally, the verbal descriptions—which pertain not only to the tempo of the performance but also to its character—are capable of sufficiently providing assistance all the while.

Accordingly, Reger's metronomizations of ritardandi and accelerandi strike me as misguided because they necessarily regard the tempo modifications as being pieced together out of sections each of which—however brief it may be—manifests a constant tempo, whereas Reger's entirely functional music actually recognizes only continual transitions between tempi. Just as in the course of a section of extended modulation in a Reger composition, it is scarcely ever possible to identify a moment in a specific key with any certainty, during his tempo modifications a group can scarcely ever be said to have alighted on a specific tempo, be it even an ideal one. In cases of such continuous modification, it may suffice to metronomize the starting and ending points. Here, too, one can differentiate via verbal expressions. For example: when the conclusion of a stringendo is especially tightly compressed, one may append to the principal indication (. . . accelerating from X [$\downarrow$ = 92] to Y [$\downarrow$ = 160]) the sub-indication 'Very tightly compressed four beats before Y'. Thus may one deal with continuous and relatively continuous modifications; in contrast, those that are effected via abrupt tempo-shifts can be metronomized without hesitation. Among such abrupt shifts may be reckoned not only sudden changes of tempo (e.g. the variations in Mahler's Fourth Symphony),[3] but also 'halting' ritardandi, which maintain their continuity throughout the repetition of the

---

3 Presumably those of the symphony's third movement, which includes a set of variations that increases in tempo at the start of each variation. [Trans.]

same motif or segment of a motif but require a different tempo for each of these repetitions. Paradigms of thoroughly metronomized halting ritardandi are to be found in Anton Webern's song *Entflieht auf leichten Kähnen*, op. 2,[4] for a cappella mixed chorus, and the Five Movements for String Quartet, op. 5.

Whether or not to forbear from including additional tempo indications when the tempo is precisely metronomized depends upon the specific character of the piece. Such forbearance is justified when that character is evident thanks to the piece's open avowal of its instantiation of a specific form (for example, a rondo like the one in Schoenberg's Wind Quintet [op. 26]); when (e.g. in Stravinsky's Concertino for String Quartet) the music is so radically devoid of intentional contents that no 'character'—other than, perhaps, the negation of character—befits it (here the absence of verbal indications has a polemical meaning; the characters are 'left blank'); and, finally, when the music is so self-differentiating that one cannot help fearing that the addition of verbal indications would do it violence. Nevertheless and in any case, it would be as premature to pronounce a general verdict on verbal indications as to predict the outright demise of musical characters.

To rectify the insufficient clarity of the numbers via the metronomic specification of 'the concepts of largo, adagio, andante, etc. whose meaning is clear to every musician' strikes me as impossible, because I am sceptical as to the 'clarity' of such concepts, at least when new works are under consideration. These concepts signify types, and their objectivity is borne solely by the objectivity of the types to which they are applied. Because the types are disintegrating,

---

4 'Escape on Light Boats', a setting of a poem by Stefan George. [Trans.]

the legitimacy conferred by their names is being diminished and certainly no longer suffices to encompass the essence of constructions that are breaking out of the typical sphere of order. The application of typical indications to works that are alien to the real validity of types—and these are the only works that matter today—could only conserve the semblance of an objectivity that is refuted by the works before they have even begun; and it would only be fit for making illusory the clear-cut efficacy of the metronomic specifications whose truth consists in the fact that thanks to their eschewal of every typically endorsed rule for the execution of a work and their eschewal of that freedom that would be appropriate to such an execution, one can specify the modicum of regulatory capability that inheres in the isolated ratio and in the severity which, solely via the precise formulation of the composer's subjective intention, safeguards the performance from bad anarchy. Or do you think it was merely by chance that the late Beethoven already often appended to the typical Italian terms an expression of his personal intention in German, thereby honestly proclaiming the double significance of his overall situation in linguistic doubleness? As schematic aids to metronome counts, the all too ontologically laden Italian words are completely useless. They are legitimate only when instead of being played romantically *in* the types, they are consciously, transparently and relevantly played *with* the types without entailing an assertion of those types' reality. Apart from Berg's Chamber Concerto, I cannot think of many works to which the right to engage in such play must be conceded.

1926

ALBAN BERG'S EARLY SONGS

An author's belated publication of one of his early works can only ever be justified in purely objective terms and never in historiographical ones. The author, whose works constitute history in themselves, is not his own historian, and his duty is not to furnish insight into his own development but rather to offer that development itself in all its immediacy. Accordingly, criticism of such publications must focus on the objects themselves rather than on their stylistic function in the master's corpus as a whole; what they signify in relation to the latter ultimately consists not in a summation of the superficial features of their design but rather in an appraisal of what remains of the work itself in the absence of any consideration of those that followed it.

It is easy to be enticed into analysing Berg's early songs in terms of the history of musical styles, given that they present themselves as being so embryonically secretive, that they are so deeply embedded in the musical consciousness of the period of their genesis; given that, like a profound slumber when the alarm clock starts ringing, they are so easily shaken to their core by the portents of things to come and so full of the tender violence of early morning that only

'Alban Bergs frühe Lieder' (1929) in *Gesammelte Schriften*, 'Band 18: Musikalische Schriften V'.

such a rude awakening can bring to them. But all of this is situated at a layer more covert than that in which Debussy's whole-tone chords are placed underneath a sweeping contoured melody; or where chords are coupled in a manner characteristic of Wagnerian chromaticism, in which this coupling is not associated with any sequences and is strictly followed through, in which it is applied to a song as a constructive principle rather than as dynamic leavening; even when a song surges past an accompaniment of the Brahmsian and Schumannian type in virtue of the contribution of the singing voice, which transcends this reposefully dormant harmonic essence, and overflows into a breadth of spiritual space unheard of in the bourgeois Romanticism of the nineteenth century, this is quite a qualitatively trivial event in relation to the actual reality of the songs. To be sure, these songs must collectively be regarded as expressive music, and certain people will not hesitate to call them Romantic and once again declare that the disagreeable figure of Wozzeck would actually be quite at home in *Tristan*, which one finds apostrophized here; and in treating them thus one would admittedly spare oneself the effort of regarding *Wozzeck* as altogether too new and strange and enable oneself to deport him to that gloriously superannuated realm of bygonehood. Nevertheless, even in these patently tonal and romantically effusive songs, Berg has not made things very agreeable to the ears of historically minded listeners. This is indeed expressive music, but who is expressing himself in it? Whoever he is, he is not the self-aggrandizing, thuggishly erotic self of Wagner, the manifest source of all craving for the nocturnal; nor the private ego, a world enough unto himself, of Brahms and Schumann; nor even the ego of the lugubrious nuance, which distinctly recalls Debussy. He knows all this and yet he is still bringing it forth; he is a youth and has heard it from his parents; he has taken it along with him from his childhood; he is using it to feel his way towards his own sound; not merely genetically but rather objectively; what he is sharing of himself, of the man that he will someday be, in the process, is of less importance than the manner in which he is stealing away—uncertainly, inquiringly, like a soft tuning fork, enveloped in the sounds that he remembers even as he is stealing away behind them. The predominant affect of Berg's early songs is *shame*, and their Romantic foreground is far more readily explicable as a manifestation of such youthful shame—the same kind of shame that can bring to maturity poems that entrench themselves behind established forms—than his lineage in the history of styles. Schumann and Wagner are quoted here after the manner in which a sixteen-year-old who blushes to mention his girlfriend by name conceals her in references to all the great beloveds of the distant past—to Heloise, Ophelia, to Botticelli's allegorical depiction of spring; and this inauthentic, camouflaged, aesthetically anticipated element vibrates with more tenderly apparent, evanescent contents than any that could perhaps ever be understood or articulated at all in actual language. These songs enact the composition of the blush that was never before intentionally revealed by music, and it is extraordinarily congruent with their character that they were kept locked away in a desk drawer for twenty years until the master pulled them out—hesitantly, smilingly and with lingering shame but also with newfound certainty with regard to their uncertainty. Anyone in search of their spiritual coordinates should turn to the works of Marcel Proust rather than to the Romanticism of the nineteenth century.

Having discovered all this we have also admittedly discovered a fair amount of substance that distinguishes these songs from all expressive music, for this shame that does not express itself but rather holds its peace—this is also heard in the music of Brahms, and even in that of Schumann, but it has hardly ever before been sited at the centre of lyrical composition, which has just as rarely been occupied by the figure of the youth, who here assimilates the Romanticism of grown men, which is not his language and which he can speak only because it is not his language. The difference between generations becomes manifest not only in the determinative affect but also in the compositional material. For this tenderness that does not leap out of itself to fashion its form but rather remains withdrawn within its own confines and awaits the form that will fall to its share; this deep and grandiose passivity, which will be expanded into the gateway of the dream in Berg's later music—this tenderness genuinely needs other buttresses for its construction than someone who lives his life to the full and sings his heart out in music, far from the temptation to sink away into himself. Perhaps it would not be amiss to surmise that the originative impulse that drew Berg out of his nostalgic reverie about his forefathers and towards *Schoenberg*, the impulse that implacably pervades the songs, is hardening, that it is showing the occasional crack and becoming palpable as their dialectical antipode in every beat, is still forcing the most sensitive sound into the tectonics of the illuminated structure. It cannot be otherwise: anyone who as a boy dreams of what was real in the eyes of his forefathers finds his own reality being expelled kicking and screaming from the dream for the very sake of preserving it. Not for nothing has the life of those forefathers become so tenderly regarded by their living descendant that it can withstand comparison with that future and completely different life alone and thereby grow tougher. Exogenously and exactingly, Schoenberg finds his way into the darkness of the songs' dream— exogenously, exactingly and auspiciously, like a new day whose dawning makes the sleeper shiver behind closed curtains.

Thus does a boyish dialectics without parallel or precedent force the songs into a new state of consciousness. A youth has fortuitously come into possession of something that grown men used to labour ever-so-earnestly to acquire, but he knows nothing about this new possession.

It is difficult to give the reader a sense of the beauty of the songs in which all of this is taking place. This is not the beauty of the secure and the skilful: at one point, one encounters the beauty of encapsulated incipience and at another the beauty of early, dream-imbued mastery, a mastery of the sort one expects from child prodigies. Perhaps the most accomplished pieces are precisely the inchoate very early ones like 'Die Nachtigall' [The Nightingale]. The song is quite simple; it employs traditional devices economically, but it imbues them with a diffident sweetness that overpowers them, that absconds from them long before it has an inkling about them; nowhere is a definitive form more compellingly imparted to the affect of shame than in the middle section of this song. Or 'Im Zimmer' [In the Room], which preserves the recollection of a human adolescence that hardly ever found the means of preserving itself. The most compositionally mature song is the one based on the Rilke poem 'Traumgekrönt' [Dream-Crowned], its hazy beginning with its felicitous unveiling of the fourth scale degree is strikingly inspired; at the same time the whole song is imbued with an economy that hails from the region of Schoenberg's Chamber

29

Symphony,[1] an economy on which the song's exuberance is founded; a similar equilibrium between structure and expression is evinced by the last song, 'Sommertage' [Summer Days], which already contains fully profiled melodic arcs. Finally, there is the 'Liebesode' [Love Ode], a setting of Hartleben inaugurated by a harmonic whim that is gently led down into an infernal darkness with that power of the unconscious that alone is capable of bearing the onslaught that Berg's consciousness later visited on the material of music.

This much will the songs say to those who wish to hear them without asking whence they came and whither they are going. They bear witness to a *humanity* that scarcely ever speaks with such purity and authenticity in music and that cannot be sufficiently emphasized in a situation that would love to forget what is human by confusing it with what is private. In technical terms, the songs are not very difficult: they may end up showing many a listener the way to the region where the fate of music is now being decided, and anyone capable of encountering them will find their mysteries disclosed to him. One can but hope that those into whose hands they fall will be worthy of them.

1929

---

1 *Schoenberg's Chamber Symphony*: the Chamber Symphony No. 1 in E major, op. 9 (1906), the work that would become known as his Chamber Symphony No. 1 only with the completion of the Chamber Symphony No. 2 in 1939. [Trans.]

ON *THE THREEPENNY OPERA*

The success of *The Threepenny Opera*, comparable in scale only to that of an operetta, makes it tempting to believe that here the operetta has been plainly hoisted into pure intelligibility by simple means and made palatable to meet the need of a knowing audience that needs to avoid being bored without being obliged to feel ashamed of the manner in which it is amusing itself. It is supposed that a sure hand has served up on society's flat banquet table the Columbus' egg of an art that is self-consistent, or in common parlance, classy, and that is at the same time consumable by society. Anyone wary of cosy consensus on sociological grounds initially regards himself as having been refuted by the fact of this success— a success that is being sustained by naïfs and legitimated by the most progressive intellectuals. One is thus compelled to corroborate doubts regarding the ostensibly sophisticated operetta form of the work via recourse to the work itself and thereby to expose its success as a misunderstanding; compelled, ultimately, if it is indeed a work of substance, to come to its defence in defiance of its success. The success of significant works is always a misunderstanding at the moment of their first appearance. Only beneath the cloak of the

---

'Zur Dreigroschenoper' (1929) in *Gesammelte Schriften*, 'Band 18: Musikalische Schriften V'.

trite and familiar are truly original contents capable of communicating themselves and coming into contact with those who comprehend them if indeed these contents do not cloak themselves in the obscurity of the work beforehand; the talk of Mahler's banality, of Schoenberg the Romantic and then Schoenberg the impressionist, attests to this. Perhaps the tension between a work of music and its comprehension, as this tension is disclosed by the work's history, inheres merely and entirely in misunderstanding, and one would be in no danger of asserting anything fantastically wide of the mark about *The Threepenny Opera* if one sought such misunderstanding in it. For the interpretation of it as a modern operetta is very much in keeping with its superficial shape. Anybody can sing its melodies, which have been written for actors; its rhythms, simpler than those of jazz, to which it owes much of its instrumental colour, are hammered home in sequences; its entire homophonic fabric is transparently audible to the layman; its harmonies economically stick to tonality, or at least to tonal chords. It initially sounds as though the road to the paradise of intelligibility has been paved with all the latest achievements of modernity and made use of by travellers without further ado; so granted: the functional wires between the chords have been cut through, to employ Westphal's coinage,[1] because one does this as a matter of course in the New Objectivity, which brazenly pushes chords closer together for its own purposes; granted: they are spiced with grotesquery, limbered with jazz; nevertheless, they, the chords themselves, ultimately remain as they are. In short, at first blush it would seem that the comfortably cultivated man has been given an excuse for openly finding beautiful what he has so far been secretly listening to on his gramophone.

---

1 The musicologist and journalist Kurt Westphal (1904–78). [Trans.]

Only upon taking a second look at the work does one find that it is not behaving in this way. To be sure, *The Threepenny Opera* first and foremost comports itself like a parody of an opera and even more like a parody of an operetta; it preserves the techniques of opera and operetta even as it distorts them. But the precise fact that it appropriates these forms quite bluntly, leaves them utterly undisturbed, as is possible only for an attitude that will have little truck with freely chosen forms; whereas of course composers of glorified jazz nimbly modernize and fluently refine such elements—the precise fact, in other words, that here the opera and the operetta tread the boards with frozen grimaces on their faces, so to speak, should make one uneasy about the work's serendipitous popularity. For of course nothing that comes to pass here can be taken from the past so literally. And even the concept of parody, which might conceivably help one to understand this outwardly simple act of quotation, does not get one very far. What sense, however topical, might there have been in parodying opera, which is dead, or even operetta, about whose sphere it is so difficult to harbour any illusions that one can expose its sunken face without even pulling off its mask?

One will descry what is actually going on in those aspects of the work that are far from being blatantly topical or parodic in intent, that are not smart and stylish, not nightclub-ready, but, rather, old-fashioned, dusty, anachronistic and trite—evocative of 1890, even of 1880. Everybody knows Mackie and Polly's love duet in the stable; a *valse lente*—not a Boston, mind you; it is as intimately shop-worn and tearfully soothing as the sort of thing that's only ever still played on barrel organs; the wheezing caesuras also remind us that there are holes in the waltz; and an amorous pathos runs riot like something from the first great electrical exhibition; the lady should be buxom and have fat, bashfully displayed calves, and on her backside perhaps a bustle or at least a cul de Paris. The gentleman is holding in one hand a crushable top hat and in the other a bouquet of artificial flowers; he isn't actually doing this, because he is after all in a stable of the New Objectivity, but the music is doing it for him. They also sing of the certificate from the civil registry office that they haven't got, and they would like to know who has united them, like in the good old *Gypsy Baron*, which of course utilizes the bullfinch for that purpose anyhow;[2] this is the stodgy libertinage of donkey's decades ago, when one's grandmother was involved in a love affair and nobody would have dreamt of such a thing. Nowadays the exact such thing yearns to be dreamt of and refuses to be parodied; as everything that is dead always lends itself poorly to parody. But it is doubtless now coming back from the dead as a *phantom*. We are all acquainted with photographs, fashion plates, from the period, as well as with these sorts of melodies; how much of the surface finish of the second half of the nineteenth century has already spontaneously taken on a phantasmal appearance in our eyes! The surface of a life that was illusorily closed off and falling into decay became transparent after life seeped away; the putrescent geniality of that bourgeois realm haunts our

---

2 Namely, the purpose of uniting a couple in marriage like a priest. Adorno alludes to the love duet of the landowner Barkinay and the gypsy girl Saffi in Act 2, Scene 3 of Johann Strauss II's operetta *Der Zigeunerbaron*:

BARKINAY: Who has united us? Do tell!

SAFFI. You tell me!

BARKINAY: The bullfinch [in German *Dompfaff*, literally meaning a cathedral parson], the bullfinch has united us!'

[Trans.]

dreams in the form of dread; art is capable of seizing the scraps of dreams, which is all that we have left of them; it is permitted to lay bare their demonic foundation, which still lacks a name, to orient itself towards it as its object and namelessly apprehend it in the image, an act which is practically tantamount to interpreting it and destroying it. This is what is meant by the *Threepenny Opera* regardless of whether it was ever the conscious intention of the work's composer and librettist, who cognized in its shape and evinced insight via that shape. In the operatic and operetta-esque form of its compositional surface, the work takes hold of the petty phantoms of that bourgeois world and reduces them to ash as it exposes them to the glaring light of waking memory. The fissures in the music of 1890, through which its content escaped; the falsity of the emotions in that music; whatever fractures time has beaten into its bygone surface—Weill, who presents it from here and now and hence from the great beyond and in a three-dimensional perspective, against the background of lost time; Weill must, as it were, substantively compose out of these things whatever time has pre-composed into them for the benefit of consciousness. The melodies from back then are fragile, and we hear their organization into metrical barracks as an assemblage of fragments; accordingly, Weill, in his own right, and the better to interpret the old ones, composes his new melodies in the very midst of fragments; he assembles the rubble of the cliches that time has shattered. The harmonies, the embarrassing diminished seventh chord, the chromatic alterations of diatonically stately melodic steps, the espressivo that expresses nothing—they sound wrong to our ears, so Weill must turn the very chords he fetches forth here into wrong chords; he must add to his triads a note that sounds every bit as wrong as even the pure triads from the light music of 1890 sound to us; he must twist the melodic steps because those simple recollected steps sound twisted to us; he must shape the stupidity of those very modulations without modulating at all but rather letting whatever ensues ensue even though it does not cohere and did not even cohere when it was being subjected to modulation between times, or in the most intricate passages of the score he must displace the modulatory difficulties in such a way that the harmonic proportions tip over and thereupon tumble into the demonic abyss of the nothingness of that method of composition that modulates from nothing to nothing. From such techniques it is a sure and straight path to the radical Stravinsky at his best; to *L'Histoire du soldat* or his four-handed piano pieces, a good portion of which also begin as parodies. But Stravinsky makes haste to abandon this formal world, to overlay and overplay it with humour and invective, and quickly seeks his salvation elsewhere than here, where there is but little space left between lunacy and triviality; whereas Weill's modus operandi presses all the deeper into the phantasmal region the more closely he feels his way along its ruptured walls; hence, he is seemingly all the more faithful in his appropriation of everything tendered to him by the old operetta form. It is in such terms that one can comprehend the shape of the music; that one can comprehend the strange, illogical juxtaposition of banal timbres, their adulteration with wrong notes, the photographic, almost pornographic sleekness of the rhythmic process, its dogged enlistment of a mode of musical expression that would like nothing more than to pour its heart forth into the void of utter meaninglessness. Something of great and enlightening power may very well result when the nineteenth-century elements in that void are joined by the formulas of *jazz*, which here under the moon of Soho already sounds every bit as passé as that duet called 'Who Has United Us?' It is completely in keeping with the interpretative form of this opera that it allows its subject matter to be predetermined by another opera,[3] and no less so that it leaves that subject matter where it found it, in the lumpenproletariat, which in turn reflects the entire questionable order of the bourgeois upper world in a concave mirror; rags [Lumpen] and rubble, that is all that is left over for the illumined consciousness of that fundamentally disenchanted upper world; rags and rubble are all that is perhaps to be salvaged in that mirror image. The operettas of the past expose themselves to the *Threepenny Opera* as satanic; this alone makes it possible for it to be a contemporary operetta. The geniality of the practicable operetta, of breezy utility music, is rapidly coming to an end.

Admittedly this is not happening by any clearly conceived design or by any means in a completely clear-cut way. It seems to be the fate of every interpretative artist who seriously ventures into that demonic sphere of the dilapidated to succumb to it all the more perilously the more deeply he plumbs it; Stravinsky fared no differently. Because *The Threepenny Opera* is both shaping the light music of 1890 in its image and imitating it, it will for the most part have to pay the price of becoming the light music of 1930. Lurking within it is an abundance of uninterrupted vitality from the realm of jazz that is relished by the very people who ought to encounter each other onstage as corpses; its parodic surface is sufficiently thick,

---

3 Namely, the 1729 English ballad opera *The Beggar's Opera*, with a libretto by John Gay and a score consisting of Johann Christoph Pepusch's arrangements of well-known tunes of various genres. The principal characters, most of the plot and even a smattering of the music of *Die Dreigroschenoper* are all taken directly from *The Beggar's Opera*. [Trans.]

reflective and colourful to make them believe in it for fun's sake, to take a slightly better but none too sharp-eyed look at it. And then there are the melodies, which they can literally sing note for note. These kiddies are quite happy to listen to it, even if whoremongers have their morals, which are laughed at because they are reassuring; and even if criminals turn out to be the same sorts of stuffed shirts as the respectable people in the stalls, who at the same time envy them on account of their licentiousness. The erotic sentimental value of the dashing Mac the Knife must not be underrated either. Ultimately the spectators responsible for this success hail from the Kurfürstendamm and not from where the play is being acted, the Weidendammer Bridge, that venerable stage prop of poems about paupers.[4] But this fact does not detract a jot from *The Threepenny Opera*'s subversive, indeed, superabundantly subversive, character. Society has many ways of coping with inconvenient artefacts. It can ignore them; it can annihilate them with criticism; it can swallow them whole so that nothing is left of them afterwards. *The Threepenny Opera* has whetted society's appetite for the last of these options. But the question of how agreeable it finds the meal is yet unanswered. For being a kind of gourmet cuisine, *The Threepenny Opera* remains a health hazard: it propounds no communitarian ideology in either its subject matter or in its music; in it nothing noble and transfiguring is posited as a form of collective art; rather, the dregs of art are

---

4 The Kurfürstendamm is a street in southwestern Berlin that in the early twentieth century ran through some of the city's most fashionable neighbour-hoods. *Die Dreigroschenoper* premiered at the Theatre am Schiffbauerdamm, only a few hundred feet from the Weidendammer Bridge in the city centre. 'Poems about paupers' may be an allusion to Arno Holz's 1886 poem 'Großstadtmorgen' [Big-City Morning] (1886), which mentions a beggar selling matches on the bridge. [Trans.]

sublated as a means of discovering the sound of the dregs of society. And he who is interpreting its discarded collective content here is entirely alone, with nobody but himself for company; perhaps they only like it so much because they can laugh at his loneliness as they laugh at that of a clown. It is impossible to play at reconstruction with any melody in *The Threepenny Opera*; its eviscerated simplicity is nothing less than classical. It really would be better off being acted in nightclubs, with whose semidarkness it is harshly illuminated, than sung on pastureland. *The Threepenny Opera* is aimed at the collective—and what art of any truth, were that art ever so solitary, would fail to include the collective within its confines?—but not at the available, existing collective it is servicing at the moment, but rather at a collective that is as yet unavailable, non-existent, a collective that it yearns to appeal to along with the existent one. Its successful interpretation of the bygone becomes for it a signal of the futurity that is becoming visible because that which is old has become interpretable. It is only thus and in no banal sense, despite its singability and box-office draw, that *The Threepenny Opera* may be regarded as utility music. It is utility music that in this heyday of smug security is savoured as a leaven but cannot be utilized to conceal what is. When it suddenly shifts from the interpretative mode into explicit utterance, it bluntly urges us, 'because it is cold', to 'remember the darkness and the great coldness'.[5]

1929

---

5 Adorno is quoting *Die Dreigroschenoper*'s brief penultimate number, the 'Dreigroschen-Finale', whose words may be serviceably if unpoetically translated in full as: 'Do not persecute injustice very harshly / It will freeze to death on its own, because it is cold / Remember the darkness and the great coldness / In this valley, which resounds with misery.' [Trans.]

ON TWELVE-TONE TECHNIQUE

Schoenberg's current method of composition seems more vulnerable to radical misunderstanding than any of his earlier ones. However much the destruction that was visited on all predetermined musical entities by the imaginative power in Schoenberg's work can be justified by the decay of musical meaning, anyone who now tried to employ a self-aggrandizing calculus to re-impose systematic order on the material would perforce be proved a liar in the light of how the material is presently constituted. For the material is decaying now as it was decaying then; no natural binding force, apart from the system of equal temperament and the return of the same note in octaves, is any longer associated with it. All attempts to derive a new canon of systematic order from the state of the material itself have failed; neither the chroma in its undiscriminating stepwise motion, nor rhythmic formulas, whose repeatability would be proportionate to the melodically and harmonically unrepeatable, nor the harmonic function of the cadence, which was decaying at the same time as the material and cannot be restored, possesses any form-conferring legitimacy. The inadequacy of all musical objectivism of the present day is owing to the fact that it presupposes a

---

'Zur Zwölftontechnick' (1929) in *Gesammelte Schriften*, 'Band 18: Musikalische Schriften V'.

store of objectively binding determinations of material that the disqualified material does not actually offer. If one ultimately tried to obtain formally objective norms by limiting oneself to the modicum of the systematic that may still be contained in the material, in other words, by limiting oneself to the pure twelve-note scale and its repetition in octaves, the result would be extremely superficial and schematic, as has been shown in that other attempt that like Schoenberg's method bears the name of twelve-tone composition and is often confused with it,[1] that indeed challenges its priority. To be sure, in order to understand in which respects Schoenberg's new technique differs not only from the mysticism of the perpetuum mobile-inventor but also every form of naked objectivism, one must not limit oneself to collecting hallmarks of the material that he penetrates and manipulates. That effort has already been undertaken with sufficiently productive results, such that the material criteria of Schoenberg's twelve-tone technique are now widely known. Nevertheless, beyond this, any analysis that bluntly orients itself towards the material is of little more than propaedeutic value. It is after all constitutive of all Schoenberg's music that although it is more closely tied to its material evolution than any other, it can never be understood as the mere enforcement of material necessities, that, rather, it receives its material into the historical dialectic; thus Schoenberg's twelve-tone technique is no natural organization of the notes that stands written beyond history in the stars, nor any

---

1 The twelve-tone method of Josef Hauer, which, in Charles Rosen's words in his *Arnold Schoenberg* (Chicago: University of Chicago Press, 1996[1975]), 'essentially consisted in writing the chromatic scale over and over in a different order each time', whence the reference to 'the perpetuum mobile-inventor' in the next sentence. [Trans.]

positive technique of derationalized method like cubism that forgets the specific differences inherent in the material. Rather, it is the rational enforcement of a historical obligation; it takes in charge the most progressive consciousness, it undertakes to purge the substance of that consciousness of the putrefaction of the decayed organic matter; twelve-tone technique is not an ahistorical force; rather, it has its proof-bearing basis in the state of the material, which Schoenberg discovered and established; it is not, for example, attempting all of a sudden to transform the material into an organizational system that would necessarily be empty; rather, it is eradicating the last illusory traces of systematic organization of that material in order to obtain space for the liberty of the constructive imagination; it is by no means a positive method of composition but rather the historically timely *preformation* of the material, a preformation that must be enforced; it is explicable in historical rather than in mathematical terms, and it is not aiming for a mathematically formal musical region but trying to make the liberty of composition possible.

The historical genesis of the twelve-tone technique is conspicuously visible on the far side of every mathematical reflection. The fact that this genesis presupposes the dissolution of the *cadential function* was recently very succinctly formulated in Westphal's book.[2] Only the 'functionless' sound from which its organically cadential essence has been banished, a sound in which the principle of the smallest step no longer has any legitimacy, makes twelve-tone technique's penetration of the material possible. But by no means does this impinge on the concrete historical dialectic that inaugurated twelve-tone technique. In order to understand this dialectic one

---

2 Probably *Die moderne Musik* (Leipzig: B. G. Teubner, 1928). [Trans.]

must set Schoenberg apart from the general chromaticizing tendency of the end of the nineteenth century and the beginning of the twentieth rather than regard him as its mere executor. The harmony of the early Schoenberg is characterized less by chromaticism than by its *wealth of scale degrees*. For example, the principle of the smallest step, the principle of the incessant transformation of every musical process into tensions of dominance in Reger's sense—into mere quasi-transpositions devoid of specific qualities—is negated in Schoenberg's music from the very beginning. His harmony aims only at interrupting the undifferentiated flow of post-*Tristan* chromaticism, at energizing the subordinate scale degrees, at out-constructing key via the avoidance of the dominant cadence. In theoretical terms the distinction between the weak and the strong fundamental steps bears witness to this, as does the concept of the subdominant, which of course has its place within the confines of the specific key and thereby likewise sets itself against the quality-lacking modulatory flow; the 'wantonness of tonality' of the young Schoenberg, which Redlich once justly noted, is nothing other than the epitome of those resistances to a musical functionalism that floats from dominant to dominant and thus from key to key without introducing any qualitative differences between the harmonic values. It was this functionalism's procedural intermittency and not mere chromaticism that ultimately precipitated the decay of tonality, as the invigorated subordinate scale degrees made themselves self-sufficient and fully broke with the cadential function; whereas the chromatic system indeed assailed the individual key but not tonality as such. Schoenberg's modus operandi is nevertheless dialectically bound up with chromaticism: he brought the resistances of subordinate scale degrees into a material that was already out-chromaticized,

43

preformed by *Tristan*, rather than, say, wielding them within the confines of diatonic harmony. To put it briefly: he liberated Brahms' principle of the wealth of scale degrees from diatonic tonality and transposed it into chromatic tonality; in Redlich's words, he 'outstepped the chroma'. With the emancipation of the outstepped chroma of tonality—which was possible thanks only to 'outstepping' and no thanks to enharmonic-modulatory chromaticism—the central basis of twelve-tone music was already discovered. In its arrangement of both vertically and horizontally self-sufficient scale degrees it signifies nothing other than the protection of the sequence of steps from contamination by residues of the chromatic-cadential essence. It enables the full pursuit of the tendency that begins with squeamishness about the repetition of the same note as the bass of a harmonic passage, a tendency that becomes greater the less tonality continues to assign to the scale degrees a position that makes them repeatable. Squeamishness about the repetition of notes, a squeamishness based on the outstepped chroma, whose scale degrees have all become self-sufficient, implicitly signifies twelve-tone technique. This technique alone is the binding formula of technical and immanent experiences, a formula that ushered in the evolution of the material via consciousness, a consciousness that was stealing itself away from the natural constraint of the cadence. Hence twelve-tone technique must in truth be regarded as the polar opposite of mathematics, as the liberated enforcement of historical necessity.

To this assertion it will now be objected that even supposing that the formation of rows is adequately legitimated by history—as is already demonstrable in the op. 16 orchestral pieces, and indeed even in the variation movement of the F-sharp minor quartet[3]—that even supposing that this is the case, the application of the rows, their reshaping through inversion, retrograde and retrograde inversion, which, in combination with the complete transformation of rhythm and the free octave-wise transposition of the individual notes, and ultimately the transposition of the interleaving of horizontal and vertical work on the rows, renders the relationship to the basic row phenomenally quite unrecognizable; that this exclusively constructive application of the material is undoubtedly but the speculative implementation of a ratio that of its own initiative wishes to dictate a systematic organization of the material that is not drawn from the material itself and that therefore constitutes a systematic imposture and a violation of the material. But the objection is untenable. Those intricate manipulations are nothing other than moments of the compositional technique that were modified so radically by Schoenberg that they eventually flared back around and into the material. Schoenberg's technique is one that after taking Brahms as its starting point orients itself more and more towards *Beethoven*; it is a technique of *variation* by means of motivic development. The weaker the form-shaping power of tonality became in Schoenberg's work, the more his constructive-variative method gained in strength and finally spread itself out so extensively over his music that the latter no longer included a single note that could not have been defined by its motivic–variative function. It may be the case that Schoenberg's compulsion to engage in constant variation is conditioned by his constitutive impulse to resist every instance of repetition. After the cessation of guaranteed repetition

---

3 The third movement of the String Quartet No. 2 in F-sharp minor, op. 10, which sets Stefan George's poem 'Litanei' as a series of variations. [Trans.]

via tonality there remained only the possibility of the renunciation of all repetition, of the incessant production of the unprecedented—the possibility of *Erwartung*[4]—or the second possibility, that of making the repetition of the same unrecognizable, of shaping the variation with evermore radical thoroughness, of ultimately pushing the variation back into the material itself. Here the dialectical streak in Schoenberg's work is of profound significance. The decay of every prescribed structure of construction necessitates the autonomous, fully wrought construction of the artefact in motivic and variative terms—provided that its related pole, the renunciation of all thematic work, is not in effect; a thematically fully determined and a thematically fully undetermined musical organism are extraordinarily similar to each other. But at the same time the aversion to repetition compels the motivic and variative interconnections to withdraw from the surface of the music as radically as possible, to move into its interior and stay hidden there. Exhaustive thematic construction and exhaustive invisibility of the thematic construction: in such a contradiction does the kinetic productive force of Schoenberg's style formation gather itself. This force becomes fruitful as it orients itself towards the material of the rows. The relational forms of twelve-tone technique signify that here, in exhaustive economy, as preordained by the row, the motivic and thematic penetration of the material is so exhaustively enforced that not a single note remains 'free' any longer; that at the same time the motivic and thematic interconnections are so utterly subordinated to variation that the same musical event scarcely ever occurs twice: that ultimately—and decisively—all of this does not play out on the

---

4 *Erwartung* [*Expectation*], op. 17 (1909), Schoenberg's one-act opera for solo soprano and orchestra with a libretto by Marie Pappenheim.

compositional surface as a modification of an identical material, that it never becomes at all recognizable as an essentially musical process but rather organizes the material behind the scenes, so to speak, before it has even really begun shaping it. By this means, it ultimately even incorporates the freedom that reigns supreme as an antipode to thematic work in *Erwartung* and *Die glückliche Hand*;[5] at the very least there ideally remains the possibility that twelve-tone music will simultaneously attain that freedom via strict observance of its own rules—that the organization of its material will take place before the act of composition begins even as this actual act of composition with the preformed material proceeds without regard for recognizable motivic and thematic interconnections and joins the new to the new in utter heedlessness of predetermined characteristic forms and yet is covertly predetermined via the row and the transformations of the rows. To be sure, Schoenberg himself did not initially develop the new technique in this direction; rather, adopting an architectonic approach, he turned to compositions that had a recognizable surface structure and unprecedentedly allowed for the elaborate repetition of corresponding formal sections. In each of his twelve-tone works, the Quintet for example,[6] there are two layers of formal construction so to speak—a latent variative and twelve-tone layer, and on top of that a rhythmic and motivic one that manifestly approximates the classical sonata form. Once the out-construction of the classical forms has been successfully achieved by means of the rationally illumined material, the manifestly audible layer of construction begins to slacken once again as

---

5 *Die glückliche Hand* [*The Fortunate Hand* or *The Hand of Fate*], op. 17 (1910–13), Schoenberg's four-scene opera for solo baritone and mixed chorus.
6 The Wind Quintet, op. 26, completed in 1924. [Trans.]

the latent twelve-tone layer becomes richer and denser; in the Chamber Suite, op. 29, playful—albeit still symmetrical—characters appear on the scene in lieu of the ironclad sonata, and in the mighty first movement of the third quartet,[7] which at first hearing seems to be held together solely by an ostinato rhythmic motif, everything is already once again abstracted from every prescribed form. On the one hand, this development seems to be aiming to allow twelve-tone technique to be so multifariously elaborated within itself that it can yield to the musical impulse of the moment unfettered by any preconceived obligation; on the other hand, the external forms that twelve-tone music avails itself of seem once again to be softening all the more in order to subordinate themselves all the more faithfully to the demands of that which is musically unique and concrete the more flexibly twelve-tone music proves capable of being wielded. A conspectus of this tendency has been delivered by Anton Webern's String Trio, a shamefully misunderstood masterpiece of the New Music that adheres very strictly to twelve-tone technique and no less strictly to the architecture of sonata form and at the same time seamlessly joins together with the radically disintegrated style of Webern's earlier music; there could scarcely be more striking proof of how little twelve-tone music inhibits any composer who receives it as a baton in the relay race of musical history.

The image that is thus yielded by twelve-tone technique fundamentally diverges from the conventional one. Twelve-tone technique is by no means merely some new knack by means of which well-behaved composers might have made their lives easier through the

---

7 *The Chamber Suite*: the Suite (1926), for two clarinets, bass clarinet, violin, viola, cello, and piano; *the third quartet*: the String Quartet No. 3, op. 30 (1927). [Trans.]

tidy compilation of rows; in point of fact, it has made their lives more difficult than ever before in thrusting back onto the material that which appeared to be the task of composition in days of old. One of these composers might fancy that it legitimates him as a composer, that it now suffices for him to organize his material in something like the way in which it used to be organized via tonality; but let there be no mistake: twelve-tone technique does not hover over the composition as an abstract a priori; rather, each row is indissolubly interlocked with the composition that emerges from it. Twelve-tone technique is the preformation of the material; with undreamt-of severity the act of composing itself has separated itself from the process of preformation and committed itself to liberty; therefore, the less one 'notices' rows and retrograde inversions the better for the composition, for compositional liberty. Moreover, twelve-tone technique is, in Ernst Bloch's words, not mathematical but rather dialectical in essence: in it history, but only history that has precipitated as an actuating principle, is giving rise to compositional liberty. In closing: the rationality of twelve-tone technique is not the bad and empty rationality of a practicable system. Rather, it designates a historical stage at which consciousness is taking control of the natural material, obliterating its stifling coerciveness, methodically classifying it and illuminating it through and through. By the clear, transparent light of the technique's rationality, the flame of imagination that is now on the verge of dying out completely in the caves of prehistory must be reignited.

1929

BÉLA BARTÓK'S THIRD STRING QUARTET

The payment of adequate tribute to Bartók's Third Quartet, unquestionably the best of the Hungarian's works to date, perforce requires a sense of his development. For all the unmediated self-evidence of the beauties contained in it, this extraordinary achievement is measurable solely along the curve of that development. This development does not proceed in a steadily dialectical fashion like Schoenberg's, nor does it consist in leaps around its inconstruable centre like Stravinsky's; rather, it describes an unbroken spiral in faithfully continuing to perform the tasks assigned to it at its origin even as it constantly rejuvenates itself. The only menace that genuinely imperils it is aberration. Nevertheless, it is precisely in aberration that Bartók essentially proves his mettle: from the most perilous undertakings he is capable of drawing the forces that concentrically reinforce his attack on the only adversary worthy of him. In no other place than his work is the concept of the experimental, which reactionary perfidy has brought into disrepute, imbued with a more salutary meaning. From the cruel precision of the tasks prescribed by his musical nature, with insuperable intensity and hostility to all expansion within the space of qualitative possibilities, he leaps into the void—into a musical sphere that he, in contrast to every

---

'Béla Bartóks Drittes Streichquartett' (1929) in *Gesammelte Schriften*, 'Band 18: Musikalische Schriften V'.

composer with comprehensive intentions, continues to find incomprehensibly foreign—solely for the sake of returning from that void to the faintly glimmering flame of the work, which the wind blowing from the exposed foreign musical surfaces rekindles. Bartók's development orients itself exclusively towards three movements, three templates for movements; just as these templates never present themselves in their generic purity, they are also never entirely amenable to being fused together. The incursion of European musical consciousness has propelled their ideas upward out of the still-ever-incandescent mass of Hungarian folk music, whose authenticity is attaining new legitimacy in Bartók's work by meeting the European attack head-on instead of romantically sheltering itself from it. The psalmodizing, motivically disintegrated *rhapsody* as a sonata-form movement with a development, the open, expansive *monody* as an adagio, the passively kinetic *csárdás*, hounded by its own syncopation, as a rondo: this is how these types are positioning themselves in relation to the developed European technique of composition. Bartók's first achievement was to pilfer these types' fancy-dress foreignness and rend asunder their genuine foreignness even as he confronted them with European musical consciousness. Then came his struggle for the realization of his three movements. The arena in which this decisive struggle takes place is the Second Quartet, where the sonata concussively clashes with the types and subdues them. The First Violin Sonata reduces the types to a common denominator for the first time and constructs the sonata out of them with sufficient rigor. In this work, the problem of the isolated condition of the types is worked out. For the sonata-form recapitulation and rondo-form repetitions, which had formerly been so persuasively successful, were no longer quite capable of penetrating the motivic material completely, whereas the improvisatory forms of folk music threatened to petrify everything as soon as they fell into the control of the pre-constructed sonata that was supposed to conserve them. It was for this reason and not on account of any new leanings towards folk music that sonata form had to be discarded; but by the same token the right to define forms had to be renounced by the Hungarian types themselves, which were no longer able to withstand the pressure of music that was drawing its strength from sonata form and smashing it to pieces. This was the situation from which the Second Violin Sonata emerged. Rhapsody and lento melt together and serve as a long introduction to a complete new structure that constructively bends the types together and makes room for motivic particularity without dissolving that particularity into the total form but rather propounding it in strophes. The csárdás turns into an irregular movement-complex, a movement-village, with a trio-like middle section that interjects an improvised air into the proceedings; the recapitulation is drawn into the uninhibited forward-oriented momentum via radical transformation; the entire thing is tied together by the principal theme of the introduction, and the early single movement-centeredness of the Gypsy music is brought home in a concluding reminiscence.

The consolidation of the types used as starting points into a unified form could not immediately be taken any further. Bartók had realized them and broken them at the same time. His experiment never subsequently found a more opportune site than the one furnished by this breaking point. He allowed himself to be seduced by the neoclassical Stravinsky and by his own past in the series of works that cluster around the Piano Concerto. In their motorism and at their motivic core, these works are manifestly Bartókian, but their totalizing attitude unceremoniously negates his previously attained mastery of inner compositional elements. Nevertheless, the peculiar venture that was his first leap is vindicated by the successful audacity of his second. Rarely has a composer more fruitfully returned to his own zone than Bartók has done in his Third Quartet. In it he takes fresh possession of the pinnacle he previously abandoned in a flying leap, and from that pinnacle he makes continuous strides forward, as it would have been impossible for him to do at the moment of that abandonment. The formal ideas of the Second Violin Sonata now acquire extensive plenitude in *counterpoint*, the spoils that Bartók brings back from his classicistic adventure in the tent-camp of restless improvisation. Not that Bartók had previously been incapable of writing counterpoint. Polyphony unfolds with autocratic high-handedness as early as in the development of the finale of the First Quartet. But whereas he formerly used counterpoint as a means of development, it has now become an element of his material like the motif, the chord and motion. There is nothing more instructive than a comparison of the fugato section of the First Quartet with the analogous section in the Third.

The Lento at the beginning,[1] like the one in the Second Violin Sonata, is layered in 'intonations' rather than expounded in sonata-like fashion; its free, contoured imitative work[2] protects it from decaying into mere improvisation; next, and over and over again, comes the Allegro barbaro,[3] but this time its ever-propulsive trajectory

---

1 In fact, the first movement or Prima parte of Bartòk's Third String Quartet is marked Moderato, and the first movement of his Second Violin Sonata is marked Molto moderato. [Trans.]

2 *Imitatorik*: By this term Adorno evidently means the elementary contrapuntal feature of the note-for-note echoing of one voice by another. [Trans.]

is interrupted by the autonomy of its voices; whenever a homophonic gathering of these voices is being striven towards, their sonority simultaneously becomes extremely condensed, and such passages stand out quite sharply from the polyphonic norm of this episode. The second section of the work is all recapitulation; first comes the highly abbreviated recapitulation of the Lento, whose reminiscing about the Allegro leaves it no more time to make an example of itself, and then a speedy coda analogous to the recapitulation of the rondo in the Second Violin Sonata;[4] this coda is a variation-governed game played with the motifs of the Allegro. The themes out of which the work is tightly and economically fashioned are more malleable, more succinct and more reliably audible than any in Bartók's previous output; the harmony is developed out of lines and overlappings of lines with a valiant lack of restraint, but at the same time this development is pursued with punctilious attention to the value of each and every scale degree. The piece's decisive quality is its *formal strength*, its steely concentration, its entirely original tectonics, which are precisely commensurate with Bartók's current situation. Hungarian stereotypes and German sonata form are melted down in the white heat of impatient compositional effort; a genuinely new contemporary form is engendered by their fusion.

---

3 Here, as in his first essay on Bartók, Adorno is merely highlighting the general resemblance of the music at hand to the 1911 piano piece *Allegro barbaro*: the second movement or Secunda parte is simply marked Allegro. [Trans.]

4 Adorno's description of the Second Violin Sonata in the first paragraph of the essay makes plain that the rondo-recapitulation to which he is referring here is that sonata's second and final movement, although that movement is simply marked Allegretto and therefore not particularly speedy. [Trans.]

The piece's specific setting *as a quartet* remains to be considered. From its beginnings Bartók's chamber music was always exceptionally concrete and apportioned among its instrumental parts in strict accordance with the demands exacted by its material. The Third Quartet surpasses all his earlier chamber works even in these respects. He has wrested from neoclassicism, which he is now leaving behind, the one thing that one would have least expected it to yield—a range of new colours. Not only is the compact severity of the Piano Concerto utilized in parts of the quartet: its counterpoint has released all colours from bondage and is adding the full spectrum of nuances to the tension between black and white that formerly dictated Bartók's sonority. He is now willingly served by these unfrequented possibilities of instrumentation as well as by the spacious harmonic arrangement of multi-voiced chords. In the Third Quartet, Bartók has discovered the productivity of colour for himself in a genuinely idiosyncratic way. This productivity not only underwrites this masterpiece but also discloses a prospect of what is yet to come.

1929

A POLEMICAL EXCHANGE
WITH H. H. STUCKENSCHMIDT ON
THE TOPIC OF LIGHTHEARTEDNESS

In the journal *Anbruch*, Kurt Westphal has lately said a few things about motoric music.[1] I can descry in his article certain tendencies that I have felt it a point of honour to oppose in every context and that I don't care to let a colleague of my own generation in particular get away with.

It is of course hereditarily characteristic of the Germans' boorish consideration of artistic (and not only artistic) matters to grant that a work is of high quality only when all the arduous effort, the full torrent of sweat, that was lavished on it, unmistakably manifests itself in the work's style and form. In this country, the habit of grabbing one's left ear with one's right hand is very much identical to the concept of intellectual house-brokenness, such that Nietzsche was obliged to devote a substantial portion of his life's work to combatting such a mindset.

'Kontroversie über die Heiterkeit' (1930) in *Gesammelte Schriften*, 'Band 19: Musikalische Schriften VI'.

1 Kurt Westphal, 'Grenzen der motorisch-rhythmischen Gestaltung' [The Limits of Motoric-Rhythmic Composition], *Anbruch* 11(7–8) (September–October 1929): 295ff. [Adorno's editors' footnote]

Far be it for me to complain if the idolaters of intellectual strain wish to interrogate one another on the caloric expenditure exacted by one another's works. But the repeated obtrusion of their system into the sphere of objective aesthetics and the application of this system as a gauge of artistic value is an unprecedented phenomenon against which I cannot protest harshly enough.

Let it be said once and for all: there is no position that is more inimical to art, and in Germany no position that is more dangerous to occupy, than that of the person who is an intellectual dogsbody as a matter of principle. And if I must choose between the genius of Mozart, whose ideas floated into his mind like roasted pigeons into the mouth of the knight in the Land of Cockaigne, and the genius of Wagner, which subjected itself to multi-week health cures in order to fortify itself adequately for its taxing tête-à-tête with his muse, I shall unhesitatingly plump for the former and let it be debated whether it did not perhaps produce art that was even superior to that of the latter.

The type of movement that Westphal speaks of so disdainfully, consisting of the brazenly motoric exhaustion of a single rhythmic motif, is certainly easier to compose than Schoenberg's, engendered by the mastery of numerous disciplines. A Rossini overture is easier to write than a Beethoven adagio.

But it must be said first of all that (as goes without saying everywhere but in Germany) the meaning of a work of art ultimately becomes apparent in its effect and not in what preceded it. Quite apart from the fact that I can readily imagine a creative artist who puts an unsurpassable amount of labour into contriving forms of seemingly unsurpassable lightness. And vice versa.

There is no more instructive or salutary prescription for German intellectuals than an occasional visit to a vaudeville show. There they will receive irrefutable ocular proof of the difference between easy and difficult art in, for example, the respective performances of a juggler and an athlete. Both our art and our criticism would be in much better shape if these people occasionally hunted their quarry in other forests.

For we have only just now arduously shaken ourselves free of the ballast of Wagnerism, of philosophical art. And now here come these gentlemen again with quite similar gripes.

It is with great regret that I am also obliged here to tweak the nose of my highly esteemed friend Wiesengrund. In this very journal, he has published a declaration of fundamental opposition to 'the new lightheartedness'. All fine and good. Sneering blockheads are vomit-inducing. There has indeed been a bit too much sneering in new music.

The cheeky optimism of this kind of art is certainly boring over the long run. But it has wreaked less mischief than the principled snivelling and caterwauling of pessimistic gloom-mongers. One can say what one likes against lightheartedness—if it comes from the heart, it has got more blood, more life-affirming strength of will, than sullenness. Depth, personal experience or whatever else they may call it: the goal of all fundamentalist melancholics is and remains negation, passive nihilism, suicide (which they, being unfaithful to their core maxim, decide to commit only in very exceptional cases!).

The only excuse for the pessimistic artist is a faith in a better world in the hereafter. (Wagner's tragedy created an outlet for the idea of salvation, a metaphysical idea par excellence.) We, bereft as we are of all metaphysical faith, prepared for nothing but a better, utopian version of this world, have no right to proclaim the great lugubriousness by artistic means. We haven't even got a reason for doing so. In a word, we have other things to worry about.

But where does this faith in the advantages of tear-drenched miens, this resentment of the 'keep-smiling attitude',[2] come from? From the same delusory notion that one is a better person when one makes life difficult for oneself. From the fear of simplicity. From the inferiority complex of German intellectuals, their sense that their fellows in other countries might not be taking them seriously. 'Excuse me, Mr Auditor: our lot also put in their eight hours a day. Just take a look at this exercise in double counterpoint . . . ' Children, don't kid yourselves. People have long since gotten wise to your skulduggery with the buskins. We want to be satisfied with having talent and being able to do something.

We are much of a mind to auction off the dignified beard of 'the difficulty of composition' and the like to the highest bidder. There are still scads of punters who would love to buy it.

H. H. Stuckenschmidt

---

2 'Keep-smiling' is in English in the original. [Trans.]

My dear Stuckenschmidt,

First of all, it seems to me as though there has been some sort of misunderstanding here. Any talk of 'work' in connection with a piece of music cannot refer to the 'torrent of sweat lavished on it', a phrase that refers to nothing but the psychological circumstances of the act of production. Rather, work is applicable as a category only to the product itself: 'thematic work', for example, is tantamount to the wealth of motivic–thematic relations in a composition regardless of how those relations were established by its composer. Admittedly Westphal has said that one sort of piece is harder to compose than another, but in so doing he is seeking to rehabilitate not the romantic religion of art's miracle of creation but rather the effort of production—this is according to him, mind you. In his eyes the artistic effort entailed by craftsmanship, by no means to be confused with the notorious suffering of the artist who sacrifices himself to his work, is only a measure of the internal technical task that the artist sets himself. 'We want to be satisfied with having talent and being able to do something.'—all well and good: but Westphal's objection, which always distances itself from the psychological treatment of music with unusual incisiveness, is aimed precisely at the rhythmical motorists' inability to do anything. They are unable to do anything not because they are finding composing particularly easy (he is fighting against them and I have unflaggingly been fighting against them), but because their music itself is not up to standard. The fact that composers today, confronted with unsubstantiated compositional material and living in an atomized social condition, no longer find it as easy to write truly coherent music as their predecessors did a hundred and fifty years ago is neither an accident nor news to the motorists any more than it is to us. So why not say so? Anybody whose experience of French music was as radically formative as yours was really shouldn't be so quick to fancy that mere professionalism is masking the odour of Fafner's lair.

Nietzsche is a poor witness for the prosecution here. In the first and most obvious place, he wrote *The Birth of Tragedy* and invented the antithesis between the Dionysian and the Apollonian, which strikes me as being quite dubiously monumental and neo-German indeed, but in any case, vis-à-vis Nietzsche's own ideal of postcard-blue southernness and classical dancing, a moment's reflection on it very efficaciously proves that his virtuous infinitude of a world of closed forms is possible only thanks to its dark and amorphous elemental foundation; whereas you are all too eager to lay down the law without further ado and in two dimensions. Loath though I ordinarily am to enter the lists as an apologist for Nietzsche, you sorely tempt me to do so: if anything in his works has any staying power, it is certainly his dialectical streak, which affords him enough profundity to discern all genuine form in the formidable tension between consciousness and the force of nature from which it wrests itself. Only once one has erased consciousness, wilfully dissolved it into nature, and also forgotten the force of the elemental, does nothing remain of the tension: in musical terms, classicism becomes a prescription for conservatory graduates who omitted to take the course on the theory of musical forms. But that would really be a shame. Mozart, in any case, if one really wishes to impugn him as an Apollonian—as I would never have the heart to do—is thoroughly and completely implicated in the tension: one needn't have particularly sensitive ears to hear how brutally and painfully this form was hewn out of the raw matter of nature—not, to be sure, out of the raw matter of his personal experience but rather out of the forward-surging material into which that music of his threatens again and again to sink without a trace with its final chord. One mustn't forget in the process that one is dealing not with intrapersonal facts but with the state of objective characters in the individual person. But nobody is guiltier of that psychological obfuscation of this domain than Nietzsche himself, who radically took the creative individual as the starting point for his understanding of all art and consequently and repeatedly falsified the truth-contents that he encountered by misrepresenting them as mere actualities of the soul. You should also refrain from invoking Nietzsche because he remains completely bound to the world of the personal experience of the nineteenth century, a world to which you quite rightly are opposed and which you are now finding in your all-too-loyal discipleship of Nietzsche even when it can only presuppose that very same ingenuous credence in psychology.

Having said all this, I have no desire to squabble with you over Nietzsche and camouflage our very real differences of opinion by exchanging salvos in the sphere of received culture. I cleave steadfastly to what I have previously said about the serenitas, the keep-smiling attitude, that is in vogue nowadays; indeed, now that the development of stabilized music has even more distinctly accentuated the prevalence of this attitude, I am inclined to say it again in harsher rather than milder tones. I peremptorily reject all psychologically grounded arguments either for or against lightheartedness because I regard them as being entirely beside the point; in connection with this one must also consider that irrespective of whatever burdens it has been saddled with, art by no means has any intrinsic need to outgrow a pessimistic cast of mind; just take a look at Kafka's novels, whose agonizing gravity is mobilized purely for the sake of achieving the optimum results. My war against the new lightheartedness has nothing in common with the traditional German religion of culture; I have said nothing about personal experience and depths in its sense; I enjoy taking in a vaudeville show as much as you do, and I am not in the habit of conversing with auditors. My war consists, rather, in a certain *consciousness of reality*: serenitas seeks to simulate a condition of objectively self-contained communitarianism, of secure ontological orientation, of equitable social organization and to wheedle listeners into embracing this condition, which does not exist; and making oneself believe in its existence by aesthetic means amounts to nothing but distracting oneself from the miserableness of social relations. I am at war with the new serenitas as an *ideology*: as a stance that is rooted not in the objective state of reality, but, rather, in certain quite transparent interests in the sphere of production; I am at war with it as the music of bad stabilization. There are no objective grounds for being cheerful, and the very fact that cheerfulness is now advertising itself as such (as it never even thought of doing in the much-lauded eighteenth century) is proof of its dubiousness: it sticks its head in the sand and stamps its feet in time with the motor—as long as the motor keeps running. It strikes me as vitally important to demonstrate all this conclusively by demonstrating the technical inconsistency of the works themselves, and it is mainly in virtue of doing this that Westphal's article serves a worthy function. It must further be said that the hurrahing optimism of the compact-car generation is in danger of forfeiting what art ultimately oughtn't to renounce altogether: humanity. That expressive pathos no longer has any room for humanity any more goes without saying, but humanity cannot be brusquely suppressed either. The

63

inhumane lightheartedness of the bright void that consists in nothing but in its own tempo, in which nothing moves at all any more— this will only frustrate the amelioration of this world and in the end must be seen through for this amelioration's sake. You speak of the utopian version of this world: well, I have found that one can confidently behave towards that world in a slightly more utopian manner than you care to concede to me.

Yours very sincerely,
Theodor Wiesengrund-Adorno.

1930

SCHOENBERG, *VON HEUTE AUF MORGEN*, OP. 32 (I)

WORLD PREMIERE IN FRANKFURT

Schoenberg's first comedic work for the stage is enjoying its tempestuous success, a success far more inflamed than inhibited by detraction, and criticism is sedulously and belatedly striving in vain yet again to prove to him that he is asocial; the audience, colourful enough and specialized only to the extent that it was interspersed with those musical score-fortified critics, has unequivocally let it be known that it was impressed by the work. To be sure, this does not mean that Schoenberg has wound up becoming a sort of composer of communitarian music for the sake of a community that does not exist and that therefore axiomatically precludes the existence of such music: rather, in his op. 32, as in all his music, there is always present the consciousness that the socially binding character of music is measurable solely in terms of its objective musical content and not at all in terms of its regard for an imaginary group of listeners that is solely capable of disturbing the inner coherence of the composition. Instead of wheedling people and vacuously leaving them to their own devices, this music keeps what binds people together locked away in its deepest cells as its mystery. Whether the

---

'Schönberg: Von heute auf Morgen, op. 32 (I)' (1930) in *Gesammelte Schriften*, 'Band 18: Musikalische Schriften V'.

work is fully 'understood' here and now remains a secondary question: the power of its mystery was self-evident to the listeners and struck more deeply than the manifest attestations of a social will that purported to be preoccupied with society rather than art ever could. Whether a transformed society, a society both free and rationally structured, will receive Schoenberg's free and rational music in preference to credulous nature-worshiping inanity remains to be seen. Besides, what does the question of intelligibility actually mean? Is anybody hoping to understand a work by counting its twelve-tone rows as he listens to it? If so, he will hope in vain, for it is Schoenberg's precise intention to strip away from the surface the twelve-tone structures that everybody is making such a fuss about, and his present work's inspired dialectical point of advantage consists in its rendering invisible all work on the rows via the presence of what visibly manifests itself in the here and now. With profound irony he has termed twelve-tone technique his own private affair; to understand his work first and foremost means nothing other than to take hold of the musical shapes, their organization, the melodic arcs and their simultaneity in acoustic immediacy. This is made difficult not by any sort of fabled 'abstractness', of which there can be no serious talk in relation to the most colourful and materially just orchestral sound that has ever been produced, but rather and solely thanks to the *richness* of a compositional imagination that in a manner of speaking penetrates all compositional devices and wields them at the most progressive level of their historical movement; on the other hand it is made easier by the unprecedented *economy* that weighs out this cornucopia of devices without allowing any one of them ever to be paralyzed by the other; it is further facilitated by a plasticity of everything musically particular—of every particular theme no less than of every particular choice of instrumentation or dramatic gesture—a plasticity that separates the partial totalities from one another with the greatest acuity and yet again binds them to one another and to the total process. Viewed in its essentially central terms, as opposed to those that would subject it to prescribed stylistic norms, the opera is as light as every great work of art that flourishes in the concretion of its own shape, and as serious as every such work that unfolds out of itself as entelechy and fashions history instead of orienting itself historically.

Anyone who found it difficult to orient himself towards this disoriented but proper opera could find his footing with the help of the libretto by Max Blonda.[1] This libretto certainly makes this easy enough; although the accusation of inhuman esotericism was ready to hand, it could quite effectively be counterpointed with one of banality. Anyone who is capable of such astonishing insights should merely be mindful that they are not unfamiliar territory for Schoenberg. The dialectical relationship between word and music whose prominence in Schoenberg's corpus of Lieder I have attempted to highlight is made into a binding formula in *Von heute auf morgen* [*From One Day to the Next*]. This relationship will be entirely, transparently visible only once the bourgeois world that is consigned to the antithetical music in this opera has passed into history. Then it will become apparent that this bourgeois apartment was situated in hell, whose laughter echoes from its wall closets, whose attendant spirits sleep with each other in its fold-out bed, whose light fluoresces on its electrically illuminated balcony, where the wife displays herself,

---

1 Max Blonda: the pseudonym assumed by *Von heute auf morgen*'s actual librettist, Schoenberg's wife Gertrud. [Trans.]

radiant with her prospective seduction of her husband. In the presence of this laughter nothing remains but the love of these two human beings, a love articulated in wretched, shop-worn words and mirrored by the music in the tentative sonority of reconciliation. Between the inauthentic, unremarkable sphere of the libretto and the violent transparency of the music lies a medium in which both spheres communicate, that of the *dream*; this is nowhere more evident than in the passage in which the gas metre reader is discussed; the husband has just come back from answering his doorbell-ring, the wife, now wearing her fairytale-style cape, acts as if she doesn't understand what he is actually talking about; she is completely removed from everyday life down on earth in her attitude, but does she actually understand what is going on with the metre reader? The music at least suggests otherwise; the expression *gas metre reader* cuts into its glassy, close light, a light that is intangible for all its distinctness, as unintelligibly as an alarm clock into the dreamy gossamer of blissful sleep; here the dream has already become much more real and authentic than the leftovers of daytime that it is consuming, and no wrong was ever better righted than when in the course of the happy ending the gas bill, a ghost from afar that interrupted the reality of the dream, finds itself paid.

The reality of the dream is that of the music. The music does not allow the dream to dissolve into intuition; it bodily banishes the dream into the dense housing of its construction; the construction of the dream finds expression in pure formal immanence; it finds it there so exhaustively that throughout the opera there is not a single breath of air left to leak out of it; no piece by Schoenberg seems less likely to be disrupted by a performance than this one, his strangest composition, whose iridescent self-containment never allows a single contradiction to seep into it. At the same time its self-containment is what makes it genuinely difficult; not a single moment of affective breakthrough affords the listener entry into the housing, which instead can become inhabitable by him only by arching over him from the very first note. But at the same time, like Aladdin's Palace, the housing possesses the liberty of the dream. In this hermetically sealed building the light surges as loosely and uninhibitedly as the current of *Erwartung* did before. The contrapuntal forms that occur are never measurable as structures; rather, they are commensurate solely with the dramaturgical situation: the contrasts and elective affinities that initially imbue the relationship between the husband and the wife and subsequently the one between the actual and the phantom couple spontaneously effectuate the musical idea of the *canon* and double canon and at the same time conceal it behind the irreversible progress of time over the course of the scene. The arcs described by the singers' voices are expansively curved and at the same time sparing with large intervals; in their comprehensibility twelve-tone technique is paying off in practically performable terms for the first time; the recurrence of the same intervallic relations lightens the singers' intonation and sharpens their consciousness of the melody. No description is capable of giving the reader an idea of the work's *orchestra*; only analysis will suffice. This orchestra decisively puts paid to the fluid, functional Wagnerian sonority, just as the harmonic and polyphonic structure that the new sonority realizes initially seems 'functionless' in an exhaustive sense and eradicates the last vestiges of relations depending on the leading tone; but here, unlike in the works of the neoclassicists, the break with Wagnerian functionalism, with its infinitesimal transitions in sonority, is not actuated by the conception of a stark, transition-free and homogenous ensemble-generated sonority that archaically falsifies the state of the material; rather, in an exhaustive, complete instrumentation of all lines it garners a polychromatically refracted, transition-rich soloistic sonority whose facets exhaustively render the lineation, absorb the liberty of the melodic shapes into the liberty of coloration and yet rigorously remain present in the composition's formal immanence. All proliferating tensions have vanished from this sonority; at the same time it never remains static for more than a second; but its life is not that of the consumptive urge but rather the movement of a salvaged kaleidoscope whose figures become legible like the illuminatingly moved lettering of the transparencies of evening in big cities. This talk about the transparency of the music acquires its literal meaning via its relationship to the libretto and also via the unprecedentedly perspicuous artistry with which that libretto is set to music. The material of that music is metallic. Chords that are simultaneously of such striking precision and such striking resonance as the ones struck here have never before been heard, and the web of voices itself sounds as though it has been woven out of metal threads whose colourfulness signifies the reflection of an unknown source of light. It is no accident that Schoenberg has fashioned a veritable system of colours out of the harp, the piano and plucked string instruments;[2] nor is it any accident that this system makes its entrance in cooperation with the percussion instruments. But this system is not starkly reflected outward; no, it is drawn into the plenitude of nuances so that it can serve them and master them. The metal of this opera is molten.

---

2 *Plucked string instruments*: the mandolin and guitar that are included in the orchestra. [Trans.]

The Frankfurt Opera has at last re-established its right to exist. Its presentation of the most difficult work in the literature of music is beyond all praise—not by the standards of the opera business, for example, but by the most rigorous standards of reproductive consciousness. The conductor, Hans Wilhelm Steinberg, is the load-bearing member of the production in virtue of his extraordinarily detailed knowledge of the score, in his veritably unprecedented capacity for realizing it so perfectly that it resounds with the genuine self-evidence of the dream. The director, Herbert Graf, masters the score in dramaturgical terms and manages to use the singers' gestures no less effectively than the set-design to convey the complete transparency of the stage-action to the music. Mrs Gentner-Fischer in the principal female role delivered on both the musical and the vocal planes—not that either is in truth separable from the other—with equal perfection; at long last the name of this great and seasoned singer is receiving the extra-local recognition that it has deserved for years. She was matched with equally talented partners in Mr Ziegler and the contrapuntal couple, sung by Elisabeth Friedrich and Anton Maria Topitz.

1930

SCHOENBERG, *VON HEUTE AUF MORGEN*, OP. 32 (II)

WORLD PREMIERE IN FRANKFURT

In the light of the impossibility of saying anything both succinct and exhaustive about this mighty work in which Schoenberg has applied strict twelve-tone technique to the liberty of the stage for the first time, restraint is needful, such that only two questions should be discussed here: (1) Is Schoenberg's present music really 'abstract' in a sense that excludes it from the living stage; is it 'asocial' and, being the esoterically artistic excrescence of a chamber ensemble of hard-boiled specialists lacking any substantial objectively binding relation to interpersonal reality, condemned to hide away within itself? (2) Why has this music that is anything but derivative been applied to a libretto that deliberately flaunts the banality of its plot and dialogue?

The question about abstractness must be curtly answered in the negative. Schoenberg has indeed taken possession of the natural material with the power of genuinely free consciousness and abolished everything in that material that has lost its binding power over us without restricting himself to partial undertakings in melody, rhythm or instrumental colour: his compositional spirit

---

'Schönberg: Von heute auf Morgen, op. 32 (II)' (1930) in *Gesammelte Schriften*, 'Band 18: Musikalische Schriften V'.

has transformed the entire range of prescribed material. But this transformation is not actualized in 'abstraction'; nothing is removed from the material; rather, the transformation of the material takes place in accordance with the demands that the material itself exacts, in the most intimate contact with its essential character, and the composer almost comes across as the executor of an obligation that the objective state of affairs has imposed on him. Thus everything completely new about the musical diction in the opera has become adequate to the material and sensuously concrete; nothing is conceived in theoretical terms, there is not a single second in which inspiration has been curbed for twelve-tone-ness' sake; in all honesty, what dispassionate listener would be capable of hearing any trace of twelve-tone technique in it? The singing voice, the legitimate vehicle of all action in opera, reigns supreme in broadly curved melodic arcs that are juxtaposed with brief segments of recitative from which their thematic shapes pliantly set themselves apart; the intervals for whose unsingability Schoenberg is reproached are very sparingly employed to produce special expressive effects; the difficulties in intonation traditionally presented by melodic intervals interchangeably employed within the octave are actually rectified by the row-technique, which enables the singer to recognize identical intervals as regular. The ensemble-worthy combination of singing voices, fully exploited in a quartet-centred finale, is dedicatedly subservient to the furthering of the immediate dramaturgical situation, deriving even the richest counterpoint of its double-canon passages from that situation. The orchestration is imbued with a wealth of colour and at the same time with a metallic self-containment, with a self-evidence in its exploitation of the individual instruments, essentially with a transparency that precisely in virtue of its sensuous presence leaves behind everything ever accomplished by Romantic inebriety. All of this is ultimately incorporated into the dramatic architecture—or, rather, the latter engenders it out of its own resources. The music follows the lead of the slightest stirrings onstage—not on a psychological plane, to be sure, but in the succession of musical gestures; multifariously interwoven with the drama, it ascends out of shapeless dissoluteness into a contour that is always getting firmer; it gathers itself in the quartet and fades away in a few measures sung by the two main characters, whose open and yet clear perspective figures among the grandest that Schoenberg has ever discovered. At the same time, via all of this the question of the social legitimacy of this music is decisively answered. For what is attained by the individual here without regard for what is being heard is not the exclusive property of that individual: the obligation imposed by the material, an obligation that the individual enforces, encompasses the obligation imposed by history and thereby also encompasses historical necessity. The good rationality of this music is ignited by the imagination; the liberty attending the enforcement of this rationality, an enforcement whose conditions are rationally preformed in order to eradicate the blind compulsion to yield to nature and effect an encounter with authentic nature—this liberty more dutifully serves humankind than does any communitarian music constituted by an ideology imposed on it from the outside, a music that forgets not only its own position but also that of its listeners, who do not collectively constitute anything like a community today; and the music engendered by this liberty will perhaps someday be better received by a future society than will today's deliberately primordial undertakings, which desire only to stultify human beings when the actual task of music is to serve as an illuminating productive force driving them ever-further forward.

The question about the choice of libretto is more difficult to answer. That the story of a married bourgeois couple who lose control of themselves a bit at a soiree and go chasing after erotic phantoms until the wife rescues connubial tranquillity with a ruse, and she and her husband triumph over the oh-so-chic spectre of the world of bars and nightclubs so that their child can legitimately ask what modern people are; that this story has little immediately to do with Schoenberg, who is a modern person in a far more radical sense than bourgeois libertinage could ever dream of—this is something that nobody knows better than the composer of *Erwartung* and *Die glückliche Hand*. Covert impulses led him to the libretto: he was guided to its banality by the same urge to which his musical evolution owes so much, the urge to banish everything decorative, everything metaphorical, an urge that in keeping with its telos is theologically inclined to contest the legitimacy of art in general—as if the utopian strain in his music ultimately would like to smash to pieces all images in order to prepare their reality. This is complemented by its thoroughgoing intention to guide and to salvage humane existence via the refutation of its perfected illusoriness; a bourgeois apartment is exposed to the onslaught of hell so that two human beings may be spared its laughter; the most shop-worn cliches are exactly suited to this, because at every moment the music directs its dreamily wide-eyed gaze at them and finds meaning in the nebulous interplay of their radiant transparencies. It is precisely the contrast between the tritest of librettos and the least banal of all music that engenders the authentic concretion of the opera, which takes hold of what the present hour offers it in order to cut through it in a flash. The dramaturgy of the libretto, its obvious situations, offer the opera every opportunity to make a big entrance and to reflect its magnitude in its theatrical effect.

The performance was virtually unsurpassable: one of the greatest and most compelling achievements of present-day musical practice. Mention must first and foremost be made of Steinberg who, as a grandiosely ascendant conductor, is the person ultimately responsible for the interpretation of the opera; followed by Graf, the stage director, who imparts the irresistibly ever-present middle term to the dialectic of the dream and quotidian existence; then there are the soloists—Mrs Gentner-Fischer, a great singer, who has made the most difficult assignment of her artistic life into her most mature achievement; Mr Ziegler, the husband, is very much her equal; Miss Friedrich and Mr Topitz as daytime phantoms of unfettered life are outstanding as both singers and actors. An audience that people tried to persuade us would be unable to understand this work proved to be utterly captivated by it and demanded a bow from Schoenberg, the master.

1930

STYLISTIC DEVELOPMENT IN SCHOENBERG'S WORK

Today the question about Schoenberg is framed in completely different terms than those of ten years ago. If back then it was still important to demonstrate that his work was engendered by neither abstract calculation nor a capricious proclivity for experimentation but rather by the implacable force of his intention, now that Schoenberg's individual law has been spelt out with complete clarity, it is instead needful to point out that it is not merely an individual law but is rather signalizing the unconstrained fulfilment of historical necessity in objective terms. Hardly anyone still dares to refer to him as a futurist in the light of a technical consistency that relegates to incoherence all music that remained below the high water mark set by it. But the shockwave that emanates from Schoenberg's music as from every form of art that undertakes to read the emergent ciphers of the changing transparencies of history with the power of incipience; the uneasiness in the presence of its clear and aggressive exactitude, the dim-witted resistance to the illumination of the material that is fulfilled in it, has survived and is searching for fresh arguments. The resistance to Schoenberg does not arise, as one might suppose, from his difficulty or solitariness or intellectuality

'Stilgeschichte in Schönbergs Werk' (1930) in *Gesammelte Schriften*, 'Band 18: Musikalische Schriften V'.

or any of the other usual cliches that are applied to him. It arises, rather, from the polemical stance that, in the absence of any explicitly literary manifestation, constitutes the entire mode of existence of his music as surely as it does that of Karl Kraus' prose, that electively affined prose that passes judgement before it has uttered its first argument. The immanent claim of Schoenberg's music is this: that now that it exists nobody can any longer get away with manipulating the material except in conformity with that material's emergence from the music's own dialectic. Its exclusivity is not that of some esoteric doctrine but that of the exclusion of all contemporary intentions that lie before it and that it sublates while these intentions, as measured by its own standards, are exposed as inchoate, frangible, illusorily self-evident. 'That can be done more simply,' says the smith of *Die glückliche Hand*—in the wordless execution of his hammer-blow resounds his verdict on the methods that are being employed alongside his own and to which his technique has curtly issued their walking papers. For all the historically significant decisions in Schoenberg's work have been made in the theatre of operations that is his technique. He has no 'will to style', as people are fond of calling it now; he does not say à la Frederick the Great in the joke, 'Soldiers, I'm your Commander-in-Chief in the Seven Years' War'; rather, the historical answers delivered by his music are invariably solutions to the most concrete technical problems. The evolution of the means takes place as a result of the urge to compose more correctly—of the requirement to follow the material in whichever direction it is propelling itself under its own power instead of throwing a spanner into its works by postulating new styles. In this constellation of the historical and the technical lies the true onslaught effected by his music, such that anyone who would exempt himself from the juridical force of its historical verdict is ineluctably compelled to understand that in the light of its existence whatever he may undertake has already been rendered transparently inadequate from a technical point of view. This is the source of all the resistance: it ranges along the gamut from the inferior soul who supposes that after writing *Erwartung* so that after him motoristic composers could stop shifting about nothing but triads, which they themselves would have grown tired of over the long run, and start shifting about six-note chords, Schoenberg retired into private life with a slide rule, all the way up to the pathos of those who venerate him as a martyr sacrificing himself so that after he is gone everything will once again be able to go on exactly as before. It is all such resistors who must now be confronted by a demonstration of this selfsame concretion of history in technique, of this selfsame transparency of the technical to the gaze of history. The accusations of isolated subjective capriciousness and abstractly programmatic musical revolution-fomenting on which all the arguments against Schoenberg centre are refuted by Schoenberg's genuine *dialectic*, wherein there coalesces a productive contradiction that naive nature-worship would prefer to write off as abstract historicism.

It is received opinion that Schoenberg took Wagner as his starting point, and the same people who accuse his most recent works of bad singularity accuse his earliest ones of epigonal dependence. The accusation takes style rather than concretion as its own starting point and is therefore untenable. Even the plenitude of thematic shapes in the *Gurrelieder*, to say nothing of *Pelleas*, has nothing in common with Wagnerian sequential technique apart from its adumbration of chords, its melodic middle voices and an admittedly good bit of its orchestral sonority. In truth even in its New German

beginnings his music is already dialectical. In the most crudely for-
mulaic terms, it cognitively consolidates Wagner and Brahms, in
the sense of effecting not a 'synthesis' whose hollowness the young
Schoenberg already fully saw through, but rather an ever-changeable,
authentically dialectical correction. Its critique of Brahms fulfils
itself as a critique of the retrospective disposition of his harmonic
means: of his diatonic system of harmony, which perforce refreshes
itself via the tonality of church music and which disavows itself not
only via its rich motivic and thematic relations but also and already
via its spacious modulations. He confronts it with the Wagnerian
chroma and above all with the qualitatively new individual chords
that originate from the latter—secondary dominant seventh chords,
minor ninth chords, augmented triads and the plenitude of inversions that are still punctiliously eschewed by Brahms. On the other
hand, Brahms' consciousness of motion by scale degrees, which
constitutes the only meaningful form of harmonic motion and
which Schoenberg firmly adhered to all the way up to his twelve-
tone period, is applied as a corrective to New German chromaticism,
which had undoubtedly enriched the available stock of chordal
material, which had brought the harmonic totality into agreement
with individualized chords but in exchange had completely obliter-
ated the dialectic of harmonic progression, neutralized the resistances,
instituted a bare functionalism via the monarchical sovereignty of
the leading tone and fifth scale degree, a functionalism that ultimately showed itself to be no longer capable of the construction of
form but rather was obliged to subjugate form to the external force
of the dramatic affect or to keep goading forward the undifferentiated harmony in the pseudo-motion of the sequence. All this had
already been outgrown in the young Schoenberg's works, most

certainly by the op. 6 Lieder. In his chromatic harmony a distinction is drawn between strong and weak fundamental scale degrees; the place of the leading tone is taken by the cadence—but a constructive cadence that goes out of its way not to achieve the obsolete cadential effect and circumscribes that effect via the valence of its constituent chords. The sequence appears not as a transposed repetition of the same harmonic process; rather, it varies that process in the meaning of the harmonic construction; the motif of repetition begins to vanish altogether under the coercive force of a thematic variation technique which, having been engendered by Brahms' practice in his sonata-form works, eventually attacks that practice's pre-planned symmetry itself; polyphony emancipates itself from the schema of the enriching accessory and is interlocked with the harmonic-thematic construction; the forms of classicism, seriously confronted by their own principles, begin to tremble; but the harmonic process, encountering as it does the resistances that the formal construction presents to it, heats itself to an incandescence to which the secure edifice of the sonata eventually falls victim. The fire is ignited in the sonata's own house; only the house's walls can fully withstand the force of the blaze. The D Minor Quartet, the Chamber Symphony and the F-sharp Minor Quartet are the stages of the catastrophe that consumes the sonata in its onslaught.[1] In the D Minor Quartet polyphony unfolds autonomously for the first time; for the first time the economy of thematic construction is fully realized; tonality stands firm against that economy's assault; its Adagio is that tonality's most beauteous threnody. In the Chamber Symphony the assault is directed at tonality itself; its organological law is broken not only

---

1 *The D Minor Quartet*: the String Quartet No. 1, op. 7 (1905); *the F-sharp Minor Quartet*: the String Quartet No. 2, op. 10 (1908). [Trans.]

by the values of fourth-based chords and the whole-tone scale that is constructed into a Mixolydian E Major but even more so by the self-assertive law of the voices, and it is still to be found solely in the iron bracings of the work's construction, despairingly preserved by the latter, but it is not that construction's load-bearing foundation. Next the F-sharp Minor Quartet, one of the most accomplished of Schoenberg's works, comprises in its four movements a kind of monad of Schoenberg's productive dialectic and fully effectuates it. The first movement surveys the formal world of chromatic-tonal construction—a world already miniaturized by its distance from the surveyor—while still remaining within the confines of that world; the second, a preview of the inferno of *Erwartung* and *Der glückliche Hand*, lets slip that inferno's demons against that world; the third engulfs the sonata entirely in the idea of radical variation and guides it through the darkest gorge of lamentation—the lamentation of the human individual bereft of the consolation of form— and into the open air. The last movement answers from the great beyond, 'from another planet', in historical and dialectical terms no less than expressive ones, such that this work seems to enunciate an allegory of history itself. This movement also launches Schoenberg into his period of virtuous anarchy, a period that is traduced by anyone who denies the presence of all the form that still figures in it, for it really should go without saying that its liberty is not that of the Dadaists and that it safeguards whatever may survive in history within itself as its secret; whereas prior to this period it was necessary to expose oneself to history's assault and advance with history instead of heading off that assault all too prematurely. History's dialectic also contains these epochs of Schoenberg's work within itself. Initially the pressure that broke tonality to pieces begins to ease up; all of

Schoenberg's dialecticism may very well be comprehensible as such a dialecticism of rigor and explosive power. The piano pieces renounce not only tonality and surface thematic cohesion but also elaborated polyphony and drift on their newly untethered chords with eyes shut, blindly plotting out the rhythm of their progress by appraising the interior of each of them individually. The George Lieder, more appurtenant to the orbit of the F-sharp Minor quartet, retain many thematic and almost tonal ties to that work, but they penetratingly simplify them by dint of that critique of the ornamental that has already been inaugurated by thematic economy and the dissolution of the tectonic symmetry of the old sonata form.

The Pieces for Orchestra, op. 16, revert to the developed polyphony and exhaustive thematic construction of the Chamber Symphony and draw them into the emancipated material.[2] They unprecedentedly evince thematic work that is independent of the ordering principle of tonality, and by dint of their technique of variation, which does not scruple to devote its attention to the most minuscule thematic unities, they establish an ordering principle of their own; they establish this principle in their fundamental figures, which anticipate the principle of the twelve-tone technique that was to come later. But at the same time, the last piece, 'The Obbligato Recitative', succeeds in achieving that transparent, fluorescent and at the same time exceedingly well-contoured polyphony of principal and subsidiary voices that pre-eminently characterizes the group of works that was immediately to follow.

---

2 The Pieces for Orchestra, op. 16: *Five Pieces for Orchestra* (1909). [Trans.]

In this group what Hába termed the 'musical style of liberty' is finally realized: *Erwartung* and *Die glückliche Hand* are this style's principal works. To be sure, contrary to the neoclassicists' description of it, this style need not be conceived of in terms of pure 'destruction'. Paul Bekker and Hanns Eisler have drawn attention to the aria-centred form of *Erwartung* as a recitative followed by an aria and a finale; Bekker has with particular perspicacity seen how in this monodrama the origin of opera and the conclusion of its Romantic period converge in the form of the lamentos. The disenchantment of opera, the abolition of everything decorative in it, even its musically decorative semblance, has driven into the open its origin—the lament of the forsaken creature that finds its consolation under the cupola of the notes. Thus the George Lieder were already grouped around the idea of consolation; thus the text that prompted Schoenberg to use it as the libretto of *Erwartung* was conceived in terms of this idea, and thus the stylistic form of opera itself comes to present itself in such terms. But nothing would be more wrong than to descry a constant 'primeval meaning' of opera in this, a meaning that once it had been accepted as a given could be arbitrarily identified in varying shapes in every historical period. A primeval meaning can never be abstracted from the historical figure of the works; rather, it is determined solely in their historicity. Thus opera from Monteverdi to Schoenberg is not underlain by some Platonic idea of consolation and lamentation on which Arianna and the nameless woman sing variations.[3] Rather, the celestial bodies of lamentation and consolation rise over the landscape of the soul,

---

3 *Arianna*, a.k.a. Ariadne: the heroine of *L'Arianna* (1608), Claudio Monteverdi's second opera and hence the first opera in history cantering on a female character; *the nameless woman*: the sole character in Schoenberg's *Erwartung*. [Trans.]

which begins solitarily singing, and of the woman who establishes her solitude in song, even though their respective trajectories are not mutually comparable. No archaic law of form envelops *Erwartung*: as it fulfils its own law, the images whose rigid eternity would always be unattainable by classical yearning genuflect to it. Hence, contrary to the fairly plausible assumption of a fairly serious conjecturable interpretation of the work, the psychology of *Erwartung*, the quasi-Freudian psychoanalytic unfolding of an affective moment towards the depths of its dynamic structure, is not a mere empty shell wherein the amaranthine destiny of Ariadne might be realized, a shell delineated exclusively by the painful portraiture of a godless reality. Rather, the space in which mourning and consolation encounter each other today is solely the psychic inner space. Accordingly, even the reduction of form in this inner space is no accident that could ever be arbitrarily corrected via a demonstration of the arioso structure. Rather, the form of the opera shapes itself out of the association of the disparate moments of a conscious process incessantly fed by the unconscious, and its total construction is in situated in this association—during the period of *Erwartung*'s composition Schoenberg spoke of the 'instinctual life of sounds'— instead of being imposed on it as a binding schema. This is where the rules of the operatic form of *Erwartung* meet their limits. This opera emerges out of the particles of emotional responses that the musical gestures terrifyingly assimilate; it is not these particles' meaning-giving a priori. Thus it goes without saying that when Schoenberg later returns to formally organized construction, this construction does not supervene as a stipulation of the structure of the whole, that it instead gleans the abovementioned particles from the interlocking texture in a kind of montage without once again having recourse to the functional organization of the harmonic complexes that is dissolved in *Erwartung*; that by means of the 'row', the regulative principle of the construction of form, he banishes this construction's virtual thematic work into the particles. Vis-à-vis *Erwartung*, *Die glückliche Hand* signifies a first turn towards such construction. It takes up certain tendencies of the Five Pieces for Orchestra; even in its orchestral sonority it is the richest and amplest work that Schoenberg has ever conceived; this sonority is more unified, more predisposed to tutti, than the chamber music-like orchestration of *Erwartung*, in which the instruments were massed together for only a few seconds at a time. The work's symbolic libretto, which keeps a firm hold on the idea of lamentation and consolation even as its symbolism endeavours to guide this idea out of the vegetative inner space of the soul and concretely objectify it, may also play a part in this. To be sure, like *Erwartung*, *Die glückliche Hand* is largely athematic. But at the same time it rediscovers the idea of repetition and no longer clings to the norm of the complete uniqueness of every musical event. During its great coloristic crescendo, the interplay of motifs is sustained by constant variation; the violent music of the smith's workshop has the contours of a fugato episode; but above all, by both musically and visually obvious means, a recapitulation is intimated, and thereby an external architecture is drafted in broad outline. The musical comprehensibility supports the symbolic expressionism of the libretto, just as, conversely, in *Erwartung* the readily understood monodramatic course of the incommensurable music points that music along its way. Nowhere else does the current of Schoenberg's music flow more fully and broadly than in *Die glückliche Hand*; nowhere else does its maelstrom draw one in to deeper depths; nowhere else do the natural impulse and the illuminating power of consciousness inter-penetrate each other more intimately than here.

Nevertheless, the work transcends itself. It is the turning point from which Schoenberg's dialectic rises up as a living, feeling body to execute the judgement of history with its material. With *Die glückliche Hand* and, if you like, as early as *Erwartung*, absolute sub-jectivity is transformed into objectivity, transformed more bindingly than would ever have been possible for the unmediated objective will. The images that subjectivity discovers within itself in its descent are the same images that it takes control of, knowingly and illu-minedly, in the end; the form in which its singular moments inter-connect is the same form with which the construction embraces its elements. This eventuates in twelve-tone technique. As the mutinous subjectivity of the opera is fading away in the expiring notes of its diminuendo of the soul's sounds, in the Little Piano Pieces, and in 'Herzgewächse', the most recent stratum of Schoenberg's composi-tional activity is rising above the silence that resigns itself to this pianissimo and that carries within itself the Orchestral Songs, op. 22, and the operatic fragment *Jacob's Ladder*.[4] To term this stratum constructivist is as inaccurate as it was to term the preceding one expressionistic. For in Schoenberg's work content and construction do not constitute a duality that would permit him to accentuate the

---

4 The Six Little Piano Pieces, op. 11 (1911); 'Herzgewächse', op. 20 (1911), a setting of Friedrich von Oppeln-Bronikowski's translation (lightly revised by Schoenberg) of Maurice Maeterlinck's poem 'Feuillage du coeur' for coloratura soprano, celesta, harmonium and harp; Four Orchestral Songs (1916), a setting of three poems by Rainer Maria Rilke and a Stefan George translation of a poem by Ernest Dowson; and *Die Jakobsleiter*, begun in 1914 and left unfinished at Schoenberg's death. [Trans.]

former and the latter in alternation; rather, they are dialectically bound to each other. The construction of the twelve-tone works merely applies a rational formula to the constructed elements of executed musical movement without thereby subordinating them to the vacuous fiat of a memorized ratio; the technique's high level of consciousness is evinced by its inner technical criteria. In this technique the Schoenbergian dialectic has not yet reached its telos. If the works of incipient twelve-tone technique—the [Five] Pieces for Piano, op. 23, and the Serenade—preserve the freshness of improvisation in their outer formal carapace by resuming *Pierrot*'s playful approach to form in such a way that that form turns serious, a new constructive rigor supervenes in the works that follow them. Their historical function is comparable to that of his three works of chamber music whose construction penetrated and fractured tonality.[5] The Piano Suite[6] and the Wind Quintet seem to be made of steel; in the Wind Quintet the bygone and seen-through sonata is exorcised as if by means of some ineffaceable inscription. Here, on the other hand, productive anarchy slips away from him now that it is entirely sublimated and muted in play. This anarchy subsists in the material basis of the rigor; but in the Chamber Suite and the third quartet, he learns to wield it in such a fashion that the constructive compulsion of the surface of the composition is entirely stripped away, shifted into its interior; and in the Variations [for Orchestra], op. 31, the anarchy wins back all its melodic liberty, to which they have lately betaken themselves in their struggle for

---

5 Most likely the First Chamber Symphony and the first two string quartets are meant here, as Adorno has already referred to them as a group (see note 1). [Trans.]

6 The Suite for Piano, op. 25 (1921–23). [Trans.]

material objectification. As of now, the last station of this dialectical journey is the opera *Von heute auf morgen*. In this work, rigor and liberty have become genuinely and felicitously indifferent to each other. Having been fashioned out of a single twelve-tone row, in the absence of any prescribed formal character it acquiesces in the dramatic moment as only *Erwartung* has done before it. At the same time, it makes manifest something that at bottom is borne and consolidated by all dialectics: the image of the real human being.

1930

BARTÓK

Like Schoenberg's and Stravinsky's, the Hungarian's arc of ascent commenced long before the War: by the time of the latter's outbreak, he was already becoming well-known thanks to a performance of his first quartet at a composers' festival hosted by the Allgemeine deutsche Musikverein. There is much about him that tempts one to draw parallels to Stravinsky: like Stravinsky, Bartók is the son of an organically agrarian nation who has wound up in an intellectual composer's milieu whose atmosphere is just beginning to soak up the technical achievements of great painting: like Stravinsky, he is making the sparks of production leap from the pole of archaic, pre-European anormativity to its antipode, the most-up-to-date form of liberation from norms; to leap from the intuited primal dissonance to the sought-after, most up-to-date artistic form of dissonance without passing through the intervening space of consonances and the European musical tradition; like Stravinsky, he is the heir and liquidator of impressionism as a mode of composition. All of this is so conveniently obvious that the historians of musical style need never have commented on it, but in truth it is no more significant than, for example, the juxtaposition of Van Gogh, Cézanne, Gaugin and Munch. Neither any composer nor any painter is called by his own name when the names of his peers are uttered.

'Bartók' (*c.*1930) in *Gesammelte Schriften,* 'Band 18: Musikalische Schriften V'.

After a rhapsody along the lines of Liszt's Hungarian ones and orchestral suites in which there are some stirrings of originality,[1] his first work with a distinct profile is a collection of very brief, drastically simple yet extremely programmatic piano pieces, the Fourteen Bagatelles. On a verbal level, they are sufficiently eventful in a Parisian sort of way: the last two pieces are called 'Elle est morte' and 'Ma mie qui danse', a funeral march and a fake waltz coupled with bourgeois terror. If one takes a closer look at them, one will discover much within them, only no Debussy. But in exchange one finds the following: the simultaneous employment of two different keys at the very beginning, a sort of manifesto of all later, much later, versions of 'polytonality'; an unimpeded stampede of eighth notes, an impulse eventuating in the likewise-much later phenomenon known as 'motorism'; a retrenchment of his means down to a single piece that progresses in unison from beginning to end as a prototype of his future barbaro style; a dash of Hungary, which is just a dash of tone-colour; not a hint of polyphony—and a peculiar, ghastly relish for *dissonance* itself. If dissonance, a hallmark of the New Music, appears as a moment of unity between expression and construction in Schoenberg's work, and as a caricature of the moribund consonances in Stravinsky's, in Bartók's, and perhaps in his alone, it is genuinely meant to be nothing but dissonance—an image of monstrousness, the same image that he has also tried to present dramaturgically on the ballet stage in *The Miraculous Mandarin* and that has been latent in every measure of his music since its very inception.

---

1 Presumably the Rhapsody for Piano, Sz. 26 (orchestrated as the Rhapsody for Piano and Orchestra, Sz. 27), the Suite No. 1 for full orchestra, Sz. 31, and the Suite No. 2 for small orchestra, Sz. 34. [Trans.]

But everything that actually constitutes his music has been latent within it since its very inception. As the same time as it sketches a quasi-ahistorical landscape, the music itself has no patience for 'history'. Its rhythm, like that of the songs and dances of primitive peoples, is a rhythm of repetition, not development. This rhythm is as much a property of the works themselves as of their chronological sequence. In the works themselves it is a principle of that motorism that Bartók introduced to music and that everybody else, including the young Hindemith, learnt from him. Whereas Stravinsky 'statically' acquires the oblique surfaces of his sonic planes from anormative rhythmic models, in rigid montage yet constant alteration, and exhibits their fissures with exaggerated distinctness in rests, in Bartók's music the compulsion for repetition takes the form of continuous motion, whose substantiality is vouched for only by the dissonant, retained individual sonority; this motion is modified solely in the syncopated accents that a foreign will contributes to the rhythm of the race like a jockey's whip applied at random to the flank of a bolted horse. This schema remains audible throughout all his recent laxly composed works, which studiously repudiate it. It may be intertwined with a certain indifference to *sonority* and colour; Bartók's motoric music charges monochromatically full steam ahead instead of layering itself in polychromatic cubes like Stravinsky's; in terms of its use of colour it verges on bruitism (especially later on, in the piano pieces titled 'Out of Doors' and also in the slow movement of the First Piano Concerto); it has visions 'With Drums and Pipes'[2] but no real art of instrumentation. It is in thus dealing with sonority and colour that Bartók has been

---

2 'With Drums and Pipes': the title of the first of Bartók's set of five piano pieces *Out of Doors*, Sz. 81 (1926). [Trans.]

most fiercely cruel in his treatment of the legacy of impressionism. If Stravinsky has turned the formerly fluid blots of colour into discrete figures and baldly joined them together in defiance of their mutual disparity, Bartók has instead baked impressionism dry, so to speak. His rondos sound like prairie fires, like smoke on the consecrated fields and wild stampedes on the plains that were once watered with fecundating rain by Debussy's west wind. To be sure, Bartók always still has a landscape, but it is a landscape that has been ravaged by catastrophes. His is a vernacular art of the monstrous; his Mother Earth is not a nurturer but an irascible goddess peremptorily hungering for a quivering sacrificial victim as newly awakened man flees from her on horseback.

The same compulsion for repetition characterizes his corpus as a whole. There are really only three Bartók pieces, which he writes over and over again in a magnificent white heat in order to fill them to capacity and to bring them to term. These three pieces are the disintegrated, loosely strophic *rhapsody*, a concatenation of intonations that he applies to the *sonata* with extraordinarily remarkable results, until the latter gradually founders in the rhapsody (this is especially evident in the first movement of the First Sonata for Violin and Piano, an exemplary composition from beginning to end; and even more consistently so in the Second); then the so-to-speak unaccompanied *monody* over the ruins of traditional harmony which constitute the governing principle of Bartók's version of an *adagio* (which is at its most beautiful in the second movement of the First Violin Sonata, then daringly dissociated in the third movement of the Second Quartet); and finally the motoric *rondo-allegro*, which is to be found everywhere, starting with the First Quartet, then as a brilliant gargantuan sketch in the middle movement of the Second, and fully formulated from beginning to end in the finale of the First Violin sonata, fused with the rhapsody in that of the Second, and applied to his freshly discovered polyphony in the Third Quartet.

The quality of Bartók's music varies with his degree of mastery of those types. In the stage works *Duke Bluebeard's Castle* and *The Wooden Prince* they are faithfully but not completely convincingly translated into a dramaturgy; the translation is perhaps more successful in *The Miraculous Mandarin*; the great pianist is less of a dab hand at writing for the orchestra than for the piano and chamber ensembles; Bartók's subsequent seduction by the neoclassical Stravinsky, a deflection of his narrow tongue of flame from its proper channel, has certainly not been a felicitous turn of events, but he is finding his way back to his own domain with astonishing aplomb. Most recently, in the Fourth String Quartet, his altercation with the Berg of the *Lyric Suite* has enriched him without falsifying him and yielded him one of his most relaxed pieces. The best introductions to Bartók's music remain the Piano Suite, op. 14, and the famous *Allegro barbaro*. Songs are situated at the outermost periphery of his corpus. But in recompense there are some pieces for children that are absolutely enchanting.

So much of this composer and of what is said about him remains too exiguous: Bartók the composer affords only one view of Bartók's music, a view of its quasi-individualistic side. A view of its collectively broader side must be gleaned from an acquaintance with Bartók the researcher and arranger of *folksongs*. He has contrived to do nothing less than wrest all the offerings of folk music from the grip of Romantic semblance and cause the relationship between their oldest and newest aspects—a relationship that the composer is rendering fruitful—to become reliably *visible* as an historically objective given; at the same time, he has summoned these aboriginal forces to the composer's assistance over and over again without having had to declare his allegiance to them on ideological grounds, without having had to use them as a pretext for misplaced retrogression. The folklorist deserves to be appreciated in his own right. He belongs to Europe as assuredly as the composer does: the rigorousness with which he is imposing limits on himself is violently if imperceptibly bursting open Europe's limits, and his dialect is on course to become the authentic language of music.

c.1930

BERG AND WEBERN

The dimension in which Schoenberg's stylistic development is proceeding is more emphatically that of depth than that of breadth. Not that he has ever been lacking in the plenitude of original natural substance, as the cliche of him as the promulgator of an abstract program would have us believe. To the contrary: no other living composer has such a plenitude at his command; in no other living composer's work has musical evolution taken hold of all elements of the material of composition—melody and harmony, counterpoint and formal construction, texture and instrumental sonority—more completely than in Schoenberg's. But even as all these elements are being taken hold of and reshaped from the centre outwards, they are moving closer together and interpenetrating one another in ever-changing ways in a process of consolidation that ruthlessly discards whatever compositional possibilities are situated at the fringes of the actual history of Schoenberg's style and yet are never fully dissolved into the inexorable river constituted by that history. The bed of this river is unyieldingly narrow, as narrow as that of a ravine, a riverbed carved out by the surface area of musical production. Every dialectical stage of his development corresponds to a mere handful

---

'Berg und Webern' (1930) in *Gesammelte Schriften*, 'Band 20.2: Vermischte Schriften'.

of works, often to only a single work; when the possibility of an entire music has been established, he contents himself with drawing up a blueprint of it and executing that blueprint so that he can immediately set about tackling the new technical questions that arise from it. Plans of entire works that are already well on their way to completion vanish when the prototype furnished by a given piece turns out to have been realized already; consequently, a piano quintet and, most notably of all, a second great Chamber Symphony, have remained unfinished.[1] This has granted his works much more important functions to fulfil than those that fell to the share of, for example, the compositions of the epigonic imitators of Wagner, who had nothing new to add to the extensive and repetitious corpus of their master. In Schoenberg's case, by contrast, the students' works are becoming necessary as a stage on which the communication of his work with the breadth of the history of music is taking place. This attests first of all to their rigorously close association with the work of their master, to whom they owe not some vague stylistic diversity and their technical resources but rather their exactingly high level of knowledge of music; on the other hand it also attests to the fostering of the exceedingly high degree of self-sufficiency that they need in order to implement in concrete terms that which Schoenberg is presenting as a possibility and which will be realized—and be capable of holding its own within the confines of the blueprint—only once a fair amount of his students' own substantiality has come to inform the conception of the blueprint.

---

1 For context, see 'Alban Berg's Early Songs', p. 30n1 and 'Schoenberg's Second Chamber Symphony', pp. 139–142. [Trans.]

It is therefore no great surprise that in being required to adhere to such a two-edged standard—a standard consisting of both the most loyal discipleship and resolute hermetic self-sufficiency—only a few of these students manage to hold their own. Whereas Schoenberg the pedagogue has exerted an influence on musical performance whose radius is as yet scarcely possible to estimate and has educated an entire generation of conductors, very few of his students have managed to persevere in being solely composers; the others have had the wind taken out of their sails by the example set for them by their master, who is rumoured to have said that he didn't 'want to raise any successors of Schillings'.[2] The foremost of the very few remain Berg and Webern, both of them only about a decade younger than Schoenberg, both of them closely attached to him throughout their lives, both of them his students and autonomous composers in the strictest sense and at the same time. If one stretches the point by adding Horwitz from their own generation, then from the outer circle Jemnitz; from the younger generation, Eisler, and more recently Zillig and Skalkottas,[3] the list of Schoenberg students worthy of serious attention as composers is pretty much exhausted. And they all begin in the most intimate communication with Schoenberg; they acquire their self-sufficiency not by detaching themselves from him stylistically but rather by refraining from giving so much as a thought to their own 'personality'

---

2 *Schillings*: Presumably the German conductor and composer Max von Schillings (1868–1933) invoked by Schoenberg as an example of a composer of *Kapellmeistermusik*—insubstantial music produced as a sideline to a conducting career. [Trans.]

3 Curt Horwitz (1884–1925), Sándor Jemnitz (1890–1963), Hans Eisler (1898–1962), Winfried Zillig (1905–1963) and Nikos Skalkottas (1904–49). [Trans.]

and applying themselves to the demands that accrue to them from their technical communication with the master.

Berg and Webern represent the extreme poles of the Schoenbergian realm. Both of them attach themselves to individual works of the master and expand these works' range of problems within their specific compositional landscape: Berg attaches himself to the Chamber Symphony, Webern to the 'disintegrated' style from op. 11 to op. 20; although it must be said that the form of the 'short piece' as one finds it in the Schoenberg of the op. 19 piano work[4] and 'Herzgewächse' was first fully developed in logically pure terms by Webern rather than by Schoenberg himself, a fact that incidentally proves nothing of any significance, as the technical remit of this style is already formulated in the last piano piece of op. 11; whereas by the same token, even in early works by Webern like the double canon *Entflieht auf leichten Kähnen*, which still adheres to 'circumscribed' tonality, Webern's pianissimo, his tenderness, his tendency to let the music hang in the air, his monologic gentleness, is already in evidence. If one wishes to gain essential insight into Webern's and Berg's style, one would do very well indeed not to take the question of self-sufficiency as one's starting point. For here the self-sufficiency is situated not on the surface of the style but rather in the most deeply buried contents of the compositions; the homogeneity of the style that prevails in Schoenberg, Berg and Webern alike is not so much imposed by the tenets of a school as demanded by a level of knowledge that stipulates the radical working through of every composition down to its last detail

---

4 Op. 11: the Three Piano Pieces (1909), op. 20: *Herzgewächse* for soprano, celesta, harmonium and harp (1911); op. 19: Six Little Piano Pieces (1911). [Trans.]

and thereby causes the distinguishing features of the 'style' to become more similar to one another. Both Berg and Webern offer commentaries on Schoenberg's development that have guaranteed them a place in the historical totality: Berg affiliates him, belatedly as it were, with Mahler on the one hand, and on the other hand with the great music dramas, and legitimates him from their respective standpoints; Webern pursues Schoenbergian subjectivism, which the master begins to dissolve in a solution of ironic play from *Pierrot* onwards, to its logical conclusion; he is the only composer who constitutes a musical expressionism in the strictest sense and carries it to a point where it turns itself inside out and into a new objectivity. But neither excursus remains tethered to the master's work; in the purity of their execution of their commentaries the original substance of the exegetists comes to light, as in the great commentaries of the philosophical literature, such as those on Plato and Aristotle; in each new commentary the new and distinct consciousness of the commentator shines through in the material of the text.

At first blush, Berg's op. 1, the Piano Sonata—which simply consists of a single sonata-form movement that does not even attempt to encapsulate the traditional multi-movement sonata schema—comes across as a parergon to Schoenberg's Chamber Symphony. Melodies and harmonies based on fourths, the constructive function of the whole-tone scale and even one of the themes (the 'transition theme'), all point unequivocally in that direction; but even more profound is the connection between the piece's inner construction and that of the Chamber Symphony; from time to time it deploys 'model themes' and attains its extensive duration as the smallest variations of the model themes stack themselves on top of one another in layers; in this manner sonata form is permeated by the variation form and the principle of thematic development wins complete primacy in the sonata. Despite this the differences are already starkly evident here. They are evident not merely in a certain ductile quality in the harmony, which often enough pairs up the whole-tone chords with major ninth chords and in general grants much greater significance to the ninth chord than Schoenberg has ever done; in this it is reminiscent of Debussy, Scriabin and even Reger. This harmonic ductility, which openly embraces the erotic tone of *Tristan* from time to time, is not accidental. It is contingent upon an essentially chromatic, dominant-oriented system of harmony that does not effectuate the self-sufficiency of the secondary scale degrees as resolutely as Schoenberg does but rather conceives of the new chords in relation to a leading tone-centred Wagnerian continuum. In the first three songs of op. 2,[5] which are less rigorously constructed than the sonata, this becomes even more evident. Certainly later on Berg's harmony fully emancipated itself from the secret coercive force of the tonic and dominant. But in him an essential quality is being heralded: it could be termed Berg's principle of the infinitesimal, the principle of the smallest transition. Whereas in Schoenberg's work, in its principle of incessantly changing and contrasting 'shapes', which reigns supreme even in the motivic transformations and the transitions of the Chamber Symphony, a principle of construction is being fashioned from the very beginning, in Berg's the principle of the transition, of the *imperceptible* transition, has primacy from the very beginning, and the residues of tonal-cadential harmony that his music has retained to this day are merely tokens of this principle.

---

5 The Four Songs for voice and piano (1910). [Trans.]

The unities that his music consists of are, it must be said, infinitely small and amenable to being transformed into one another at will and in infinitely small proportions; their differences must be disregarded: in this respect Berg's music resembles an entity that unfolds much in the manner of a plant. Its schema is that of the *organism*, whereas in Schoenberg's music the organic entity is dialectically paralyzed by the motif of construction from the very beginning. This 'organic' entity in Berg's music is what connects him to the nineteenth century and to Romanticism—his task presented itself to him in such a way that it was illuminated gradually, comprehended in tectonic terms without threatening to banish nature, which in his work is originally represented as dark, amorphous, unconsciously ever-growing and dreamlike. None of this is alien to Schoenberg; *Erwartung* has plenty of it, and both composers converge here with elements of psychoanalysis, which was not conceived in Schoenberg and Berg's hometown by chance. But in Berg's work this is all far more undialectical, more passive—more Schubertian, one might almost say—than in Schoenberg's and is therefore less overcome in violent dynamism than sublimated in ever-progressing knowledge. The first stage of this progress is the String Quartet, op. 3. Harmonically less dependent on the leading tone than the sonata, thematically looser and unhampered by sequences thanks to incessant variation, it develops the principle of the smallest transition via the most intricate motivic division: often the themes are reduced to an individual note that ties them to the ensuing motivic unity; the thematic 'remnant' resulting from such reduction, a remnant that fits itself into every transition, is its principal formal medium; even the formal structure of the whole keeps clinging to certain harmonic complexes in a scaled-back technical register instead of incessantly introducing fresh scale degrees like Schoenberg. Just as the interval of the semitone, the leading tone, binds everything together as the smallest unity in the earliest works, here the motivic particle is the binding force. Then in the Pieces for Clarinet and Piano the intention of the smallest motivic unity leads to a diminution of the formal space itself: Berg is seemingly drawing closer to the Webernian expressive miniature. But only seemingly, for Webern's miniatures derived their formal legitimacy from the uniqueness of all their motivic elements, whereas Berg adheres to the principle of motivic transition even in the clarinet pieces and thereby institutes a dynamism that requires the larger-scale forms, because in them the motivically unique element never has the character of definitiveness that Webern assigns to it. And so it is not at all surprising that his very next work, the *Altenberg Lieder*, is already coming to grips with prescribed forms; that Berg's path, which at one point intersected with Webern's, is now following an entirely different trajectory. The *Altenberg Lieder* already contains a passacaglia that anticipates the formal principles of *Wozzeck*. At the same time Berg conquers the full concert orchestra here. The composition that originated next, the Three Pieces for Orchestra—which was dedicated to Schoenberg, is one of Berg's principal works, and has yet to be as well-known as it deserves—already displays his complete mastery of the orchestra. In this work Berg's productive encounter with Mahler is fulfilled. Mahler's symphonic sprawl, his concentration of the brass groups, the choric abundance of his woodwind passages, are apperceived; even the rhythmic imprint of the motifs makes reference to him; but all of this is transferred to a completely freehanded treatment of harmony dominated by multi-note chords and to a polyphonic style whose plenitude is scarcely matched even by Schoenberg. All the while, Berg's specific modus operandi, the construction of a piece out of the smallest particles and in the smallest transitions, is strictly safeguarded; the entire Präludium is already designed as a single instance of retrograde motion, like the Adagio of the Chamber Symphony later on. The finale, the March, whose chordal polyphony has yet to meet its rival, is quite simply overwhelming. The middle piece—the last one composed—a 'Round-Dance' in the sense that Mahler's scherzos are round-dances, already evinces a certain clarifying dilution of the sonic image, which is subsequently distilled into complete transparency in *Wozzeck*. In *Wozzeck*, an original and central conception allows Berg's formal elements to achieve complete equilibrium. The hollow, unconscious and vegetable plenitude is pressed into the service of depicting the hollow and unconscious essence of the human individual; likewise in compliance with the dictates of the dramatic idea, the Mahlerian folk music that was in conflict with freehanded atonality turns into a subterranean folk music of the dream that is shown in its true light only thanks to the dissonant character of the harmony and the orchestra's dimmed forte dynamics; the psychological impetus of Berg's music and the rigor of its construction unite in the dramatic form, in which every moment strives to be psychologically apt, unique and unrepeatable, while at the same time the totality is through-composed: a suite, a rigorously composed symphony whose colossal scherzo is the tavern scene, a series of five 'inventions', that occasionally thrusts a specific moment of compositional technique into the foreground—this comprises the musical form of *Wozzeck*, which at the same time retains leitmotivic interconnections and thanks to its ruthless art of variation enjoys the liberty of following the dramatic movement at will. Musical forms such as the fugue, the passacaglia, the Lied and the march, are fully organically integrated into the work. This is not the place in which to analyse its plot in its entirety. What establishes *Wozzeck*'s legitimacy decisively is its *tone*: the sound of the downtrodden human individual banished into the dark realm of his own dreams, a man who, in perishing without hope, issues a call for the transformation of human existence. After completing the opera, which is quite simply the greatest dramatic work in the entire corpus of the new music, Berg returned to the domain of purely instrumental music. In the Chamber Concerto the constructive results of *Wozzeck* are transferred to an idea conceived in a spirit of play: the work begins with a set of variations for piano and winds; these are replied to by the symmetrically retrograde-form Adagio with violin; the two movements contrapuntally constitute the finale, the Rondo. The work's colossal dimensions are mastered with sovereign power; even its most audacious combinatorics retains its transparency, and the expressive profundity of *Wozzeck* becomes instrumentally fruitful. It becomes even more fruitful in the *Lyric Suite* for string quartet, the most intimate and close-grained piece that Berg has written so far. It, too, has its central formal idea: the unfolding of extremes. It introduces three pairs of movements: the first pair, an Allegretto and Andantino, are still fairly similar to each other in their lyrical tenderness; in the next, the fugitively whispered Allegro and the passionate Adagio, the tension is heightened through the sharpening of contrasts; in the last, the work is propelled to its catastrophe in the demonic Presto and an inconsolable Largo that expires without actually ending after its final outburst. The work's expressive construction complements its material construction, which derives its contrasts from twelve-tone technique and free atonality. It is deeply characteristic of Berg that for all its rigorousness, the twelve-tone technique of the last movement leaves room for a quotation from *Tristan*, with which Berg once again evokes his own roots. The *Suite* surpasses even *Wozzeck* in point of concentration and thematic substance and is guaranteed to make the most immediate possible impact. It was followed by a pure twelve-tone work in the form of 'Der Wein', a concert-aria setting of a Baudelaire poem. A second great opera is in progress, and like the first it takes its subject from a great literary work: Wedekind's *Lulu* diptych.

Like Berg, Webern is connected with the earlier Schoenberg— but not with the Chamber Symphony's master of variation; rather, with the harmonist of the older vocal music with its wealth of scale degrees. If Berg transfers Schoenberg's motivic technique to cadential harmony, Webern inherits from Schoenberg his outright circumscription or avoidance of the cadence. Accordingly, his music contains not a trace of Berg's dynamism; rather, his works resemble windowless monads; it is no accident that they, and in particular the mature works, cleave to pianissimo as their baseline dynamic indication. His op. 1, the Passacaglia, is already a masterpiece; the piece for a cappella choir, op. 2, sublimates the technique of Schoenberg's 'Friede auf Erde' in its ethereally hovering sonority. The George Lieder, op. 3,[6] with an entirely covert tonality in their background, comport themselves in much the same way as Schoenberg's George Lieder; they dissolve the latter's contours in

---

6 *Fünf Lieder aus 'Der seibente Ring'* [Five Lieder from Stefan George's *The Seventh Ring*] (1908–9). [Trans.]

arabesques, and in their disembodied piano writing they explicitly expose Webern to full view. The next cycle, op. 4,[7] likewise consisting of settings of George, with its magnificent 'Welt der gestalten lang lebewohl', is somewhat more material; here, in return, his harmonic breakthrough takes place and his characteristic profiling of the vocal line comes into its own. Of the *Five Movements* for string quartet, op. 5, the first invites comparison to Berg's Piano Sonata. It is a sonata-form movement: like Berg's opus it is on the whole rigorously constructed out of the interplay of themes. But whereas in Berg the construction is manifest and ties the sections together, here it is hidden; from the very beginning the variation technique is dealt with in such a way that the ear is scarcely capable of immediately perceiving motivic relations; rather, it is confronted by an uninterruptedly fresh production of themes whose thematic organization is actualized in a manner that is almost imperceptible by the listener. This is why the dimensions are incomparably smaller; the first piece totals just over fifty measures; the 'normal' quartet sonority is pushed to its utmost limits—apportioned among pizzicati, harmonics and col legno effects—and thereby annihilated; the themes are split into particles, but unlike Berg's particles, which are stacked on top of one another in expansive layers, all of these remain unique, binding and definitive in their own right. In the four succeeding pieces the dimensions of the form are fully contracted to those of the miniature. Like, for example, Schoenberg's [Five] Pieces for Orchestra, op. 16, these movements are no strangers to motivic work, but they no longer tolerate an external formal structure in the traditional sense. Even the Lied form is only ever-so-briefly hinted at in them. They

---

7 *Five Lieder* (1908–9). [Trans.]

are already engaged in the shaping of expressionistic miniaturism, to which Webern was to remain loyal for a long time. This loyalty is already distinctly evident in the Six Pieces for Orchestra, op. 6, with its harrowing funeral march, in which Webern joins forces with Mahler for the first and last time and in his own way. The next group of works is entirely athematic like Schoenberg's *Erwartung*; it remains confined to minuscule dimensions; it disestablishes the material until only the breath, the sign, is left; the Four Pieces for Violin and Piano, op. 7, still effect this disestablishment with melodic interconnections; it is effected in a completely logical manner, with the overwhelming magnitude of the smallest quantity, in the Six Bagatelles for string quartet, op. 9, and the Five Pieces for Orchestra, op. 10, which still dab the disparate notes against one another in twilit tenderness and completely and monologically subsume the music under solitary inwardness, but in virtue of bearing the stamp of this inwardness, they acquire such purity of conception that the isolated music paradoxically possesses a potency of great poignancy. In the Three Little Pieces for Cello and Piano, op. 11, the turning point in Webern's development, the music shrinks to a single point, loses its temporal dimension. From this point it arises afresh—propped up by the poetic word, which alone is capable of carrying it forward from here. The Four Lieder for Voice and Piano, op. 12, display long—and incidentally often quite curiously simple—arcs; their simplicity and expressive power taste like the sweetness that leaks out of the shrivelled fruit of the preceding instrumental works. The Chamber Lieder, op. 14,[8] witness the fulfilment of Webern's encounter with the poet Trakl, with whom he

---

8 Six Lieder After Poems by Georg Trakl for voice, clarinet, bass clarinet, violin and cello (1921). [Trans.]

is more closely affined than with any other, even if he surpasses the poet of the forsaken anechoic self via the strength of the form-constituting objectification with which he overcomes solitude as he continues shaping it all the way to the end. The last song concludes with the words 'Compassion of radiant arms / encircles a breaking heart'—nothing could more faithfully encapsulate the tone of Webern's music, which leans into the abyss of mourning to prepare itself for hope's bottomless plunge. After the lyricism of the Trakl Lieder, probably his most accomplished work, this Kierkegaardian streak in Webern—a Kierkegaardian despite his Catholicity, just as he owes something decisive to Karl Kraus, the unique individual par excellence—begets a group of religious compositions whose inwardness distinguishes them from all official sacred music, as does the radicalism of their style, which despite the Latin texts manages to do without any trace of an inclination towards archaism, to do without the fiction of a singing congregation. Five Scared Songs for Voice and Instruments, op. 15, is the principal work of the group.[9] In two extraordinarily difficult vocal cycles—Three Lieder for Voice, E-flat Clarinet and Guitar, op. 18, and Two Lieder for Mixed Choir and Chamber Ensemble on texts by Goethe, op. 19—Webern's constructive will discovers twelve-tone technique. They are difficult in a twofold sense: for the performers, on account of the large intervals that Webern brings to twelve-tone technique; and for the composer, because in them he discovers the task of maintaining his disintegrated style—which dispenses with every foothold afforded by the compositional surfaces, and which is a complete stranger to every kind of sequence, to every form of rhythmic repetition in

---

9 The instruments are flute, clarinet, trumpet, harp, and viola. [Trans.]

general—in the face of the exigencies of twelve-tone technique. He has accomplished this task: scholarly analysis alone, not the acoustic impression, allows one to distinguish Webern's twelve-tone works from his earlier ones; he has so to speak belatedly filled in the fissure between freehanded atonality and twelve-tone technique that Schoenberg's dialectic carves out. Then, the moment he attains a free command of twelve-tone technique—free with regard to his personal expression—he returns to instrumental music and now finally, for the first time since his op. 1, he again betakes himself to the larger dimensions that twelve-tone technique makes available to him, and yet he does not thereby diminish the definitive character of the individual motivic event. The two-movement String Trio, op. 20, one of the masterpieces of the new music, serves in many respects as a companion piece to Berg's *Lyric Suite*. Just as Berg achieved a Webernian tenderness of sonority, a Webernian espressivo of the particular, in that work, in his Trio, Webern has acquired an ability to wield extended forms that is equivalent to Berg's. Thus, at the height of their development as composers, as in the beginning, the two masters are becoming more like each other and demonstrating the objective truth-content of a style that is not exhausted by the results of individual decisions. A slow, intrinsically flexible, tenderly fluid movement constitutes the first part of the work; its finale has a sonata movement-like character and eventually melts the sonata scheme down completely in the expression of subjective freedom without relinquishing the scheme's characteristic features to even the slightest extent: it is quite simply the prototype of a contemporary sonata that has proved its validity. His sovereign command of the material then leads to the astonishing simplification of his entire style in the Symphony, op. 21. It is a symphony only in a very limited sense, in its employment of an orchestral apparatus—a small one—and a certain objective bearing of the whole that starkly contrasts with Webern's expressionistic technique without estranging itself from its origins in that technique. The first movement is an exceedingly intricate double canon; the second features variations on a wholly tender, relaxed theme that is concentrated and simplified via a series of bewildering combinations and produces repetitions of groups even indirectly. By the most complicated means the entire work conveys an impression of compelling, naturally fluid self-evidence. Its dimensions remain very terse. A new, spacious work, a quartet for a specially selected combination of instruments,[10] has just rounded off his output to date.

Such is the developmental trajectory of these two coequal masters. In their unstinting fulfilment of their historical mission as composers, Schoenberg's pupils have become his heirs, who cultivated their innate possessions to maturity and are now using them to push their inheritance ever closer to the dark, scarcely dreamt-of and yet certain goal of all music. The fulfilment of the history of music could not be in better hands than theirs.

1930

---

10 The Quartet for Violin, Clarinet, Tenor Saxophone and Piano, op. 22 (1930). [Trans.]

AN INITIATE'S REPLY

TO HANS F. REDLICH

Dear Dr Redlich:

If I am determined to make a few public observations on your theses on Schoenberg as 'the Great Untimely One',[1] I am likewise impelled by an awareness that I have been disburdened of the fruitless effort of engaging in the sort of polemic that hopes to persuade its adversary in the absence of the remotest possibility of doing so. In your case, what is necessary is not to persuade the adversary but to remind him. Although it is certain that you, like every other writer, enjoy the right to change your opinions, it is no less certain that you will be disinclined to interpret this right as the right to forget hard-won knowledge at the drop of a hat. But it seems to me as if many of your very own earlier insights would be well served by casting Schoenberg's work in a different light than the mundane and everyday light to which you are now lending

---

'Antwort eines Adepten' (1934) in *Gesammelte Schriften*, 'Band 18: Musikalische Schriften V'.

1 Adorno's reply is to Hans F. Redlich's article 'Der große Unzeitgemäße. Gedanken zu Arnold Schönbergs 60. Geburtstag' [The Great Untimely One: Thoughts on Arnold Schoenberg's Sixtieth Birthday] in the 25 October 1934 issue of Viennese music magazine *23*. [Translator's note, based on an editors' note in Adorno's *Gesammelte Werke* (Complete Works)]

your support as if that work had not long since assimilated all the lineaments of strangeness and had instead effected a conformism that ought to be as suspicious-looking to you as it is to me. The casting of this light would simply entail extending those insights— technological insights in the best and most proper sense of the word—to their logical telos. Now you have asserted that Schoenberg is a revolutionary 'only in virtue of the constant consistency of his uncompromising itinerary' and thereby evinced scepticism about the value of consistency itself. But I am unfamiliar with any revolution that ever could have taken any other form than that of consistency—in other words, any revolution that ever could have emancipated itself from the existent in its historical actuality; and since it seems to me that every other mode of effecting revolution, every purportedly radical attempt to begin afresh at the very beginning, is but shabbily utopian in essence and most often merely a relapse in the conditions of production, conditions whose substance cannot be reconstituted out of pure immediacy, I must at least insist on consistency until I set eyes on a version of inconsistency whose own truth-content proves to be authentic.

Please accordingly allow me to touch on the dubiousness of the word *untimely* itself: its truth content is certainly not of sufficient magnitude to compel anyone to renounce a commitment to consistency. Two different things are put in play via this talk of 'the untimely': a vague and inarticulate concept of 'the' epoch, a concept that leaves room for mutually contradictory assertions; and a concept of the individual as an entity who is fundamentally independent of that selfsame epoch, a naked abstraction that can withstand as little scrutiny in Schoenberg's case as in Mahler's, an abstraction that can

itself be devised only in extremely individualistic pre-extant conditions and that in your words hails from the 'deepest depths of the
nineteenth century', a century in conjunction with which, according
to you, the very possibility of employing the term unfolded. Not
by chance, the term in its incisive form owes its origin to Nietzsche.
To be sure, in his works, it figured ironically: it was employed in
order to guarantee the liberty and profundity of the artist in face of
the bourgeoisie's inculcation of the inertia and conventionality that
the first of the *Untimely Meditations* so exemplarily attacked in the
person of the philistine David Friedrich Strauss. But I need not tell
you, the perspicacious critic of Stravinsky, how risky it is to flag
aggressively ironic categories as 'positive' without a moment's fore-
thought. But the concept loses every appearance of legitimacy when
one takes stock of what a sweeping turn the two fronts have taken
in relation to each other since Nietzsche's youth. He saw the philistine as the utilitarian believer in progress, the caricature of the
Hegelian dialectician; but the philistines—who admittedly survived
Nietzsche's fate unchallenged—have long since appropriated his
own arguments and values; for the longest time every petit-bourgeois
stuffed shirt has known that it is not the done thing to believe in
progress and that if one repudiates this belief, one must aim to be
taken simultaneously for a guardian of culture and a respectable
man with a reliably correct cast of mind; Nietzsche's untimeliness
has long since turned into timeliness and all talk of timeliness into
empty cliche; amid such confusion is it not inevitable and understandable that this talk of the timely and the untimely should
abrogate every binding obligation and render itself employable
willy-nilly, as a mere ornament?

For this reason, I naturally balk at the very substance of your theses. It is to little purpose indeed to state that Schoenberg hails from 'the deepest depths of the nineteenth century'; for although you can readily trace the stylistic moment of 'expression' and the technical moment of chromaticism back to the 'late Romanticism' of that period, I could no less readily describe the criticism of the musical language that Schoenberg was already beginning to practice in his early works (and in which, incidentally, I descry his most profound affinity with Karl Kraus), his war on ornamentation, his programmatic insistence that music must not be decorative but true—I could describe all of this as being most fundamentally a war on 'late Romanticism' or simply on Strauss and Reger: Schoenberg is in point of fact and in every sense *the* dialectical composer.

But please allow me rather to inquire exactly how you expect to bring your thesis on the deepest depths of the nineteenth century to substantive fulfilment. This thesis is twofold—first it states that the nineteenth century's 'naively optimistic belief in progress' is manifesting itself in Schoenberg; and next that he has sublimated that century's 'artistic materialism' as a 'joyful overestimation of material effects in art' into a 'hedonistic sonic aesthetic of the most refined equilibrium'—but by the very same token it is dichotomous. Regarding the aforementioned naive belief in progress, it seems to me that, as I said, in today's world it would be more honourable to defend it than to relinquish it in a joyous overestimation of the probative force of the current juste milieu. All the same, one must keep an eye on what is being referred to as progress. The belief that composers keep composing better and better and have 'overcome' Beethoven is one that I trust you would never seriously ascribe to

Schoenberg; but it is quite seriously entertained by those cheerful gentlemen who believe that they are ever-so-rapidly overtaking Schoenberg as an 'evolutionary moment', and there is no way of plausibly arguing that Schoenberg's historically decisive works— say, from the F-sharp minor quartet to *Pierrot*—breathe that 'optimistic' spirit; in these very works, Schoenberg's violence forced open a subkingdom of anxiety, anguish and demonism into which music shone down for barely seconds at a time before him; anyone who has ever truly beheld the features of this music, whose formal objectivity often seems to be nothing other than that of the expression, now congealed into rigor mortis, of imperilled being itself as it falls silent in its agony and speaks only thanks to the power of muteness—any such person will be wary of palpating the silence of this music with phrases like 'optimistic belief in progress'. 'Faith in progress' can be spoken of in connection with Schoenberg only in one specific and very precise sense—in the sense that his music aims at the progressive liberation of consciousness in relation to the latter's musical material: this as consciousness ever more thoroughly penetrates the material, takes possession of it, exorcises its mythical alienness and finally begins to echo back from the completely subjugated material itself. This is precisely what you yourself term 'artistic materialism'. But here you do violence to these words: materialism must never be understood as the illuminative penetration and emancipation of the material in the absence of all mediating theory; but you employ the word equivocally, as the logicians would put it, and take advantage of the usual aversion to materialism—is this not the pet aversion of *today's* philistine?—in order to condemn progress in the *subjugation* of the material. I don't know what other effects art could ever be capable of other than its 'material effects', given that it only ever manifests itself as shaped material; but to the extent that, as Cézanne put it, the ambition of every artist is to 'realize' something, its 'material effect' can never be overestimated by him either joyfully or sorrowfully. But if you are insinuating that Schoenberg overestimates the effect of the 'material in itself', in other words the material considered independently of the power with which it is subjugated, your demurral is objectively misdirected. It is misdirected precisely because joy in the sensuous 'sound', in unmediated 'music-making', in the various aspects of instrumental performance as naked, reified aspects of the material 'in itself'—all these things are hallmarks of the very vectors to which Schoenberg is diametrically opposed. Their advocates are in the habit of pejoratively calling Schoenberg 'abstract'; you instead term him a 'hedonist'; and my certainty of conviction that the 'Red Mass' in *Pierrot* ultimately *sounds* more beautiful than Stravinsky's Black Mass is matched by the paucity of evidence of hedonism provided by this sonic resemblance. Hedonism is a moral concept, not an aesthetic one; no version of art can comport itself towards sensual pleasure as such, via which art itself established its original relation to human beings, except in a 'sublimating' fashion; but if you would actually be so unprecedentedly and startlingly radical as to promote the complete emancipation of 'pleasure', human beings would also necessarily demand the 'revelations from another dimension' that Schoenberg would be popularly compared to and that 'the' youth to whom you are appealing wouldn't have the faintest notion what to do with. In one fell swoop human beings would become the very 'untimeliness' whose function you evince little inclination to take on.

Now you seem to want to give greater specificity to this talk of the 'hedonist', which at least possesses the advantage of complete and joyous novelty, via its connection with *chromaticism*, which, according to you, if I'm completing your thoughts correctly, belongs exclusively to the sphere of erotic pleasure and confines music to this sphere. But it is at precisely this point that I must put you in mind of your own writings, which you yourself quote. Have you yourself, and precisely in your outstanding essay on Schoenberg's tonality, not proved that he is incapable of being extrapolated without further ado from the tendency towards ever-greater chromaticism, as the cliched view would have it, that indeed his relation to this tendency has been fraught with tension from the very beginning; have you not trenchantly and correctly spoken of the 'wantonness of tonality' of his earlier works and demonstrated that the transition to independence of his new chords is precisely *not* explicable in terms of the principle of the leading tone, but rather in terms of the transference of the consciousness of scale degrees—of Brahms' consciousness thereof, if you will—into chromaticism; was it not you who coined the term 'the outstepped chromatic semitone'? But did you not thereby define Schoenberg at his harmonic starting point as a dialectical counterpoise to the 'deepest depths of the nineteenth century', and specifically to Wagner; and did you not define him as a dialectical counterpoise because he simultaneously pursued the chromatic principle and interrupted it via resistances to it in order to 'sublate' it in the end? And now that I'm reminding you of these things, I may as well ask: have you not also, in your article on the chorale preludes, pointed out the compulsiveness inherent in Schoenberg's instrumentation; a compulsiveness that you, in complete agreement with my intentions, inferred from the gradual extinction of the organ, and that prompted you, in your analysis of that selfsame instrumentation, to highlight the necessity of this modus operandi as a contrast to mere individualistic joyousness? Are you recanting this—or do you believe it can be brought into agreement with your theses? That would be difficult to do.

This is not the place for sociological analysis. Accordingly, I shall say only this much regarding your second argument: the empirical reception of an art implies nothing about its inner social structure, a structure that in Schoenberg's case inheres in the very movement of material that you term 'materialistic'. For this material is no mere natural material; rather, it is historical in the eminent sense, and in the artist's conflict with it his conflict with society is fulfilled; the image of society that lives in this conflict may admittedly be fundamentally different from that of present-day society; but it may reveal more about a future society and do so more precisely than those products that you yourself have termed products of warmed-over secondhand Romanticism, or even those neoclassical compositions whose inauthenticity you previously rendered undoubtable. Nevertheless, it seems more significant to me that in your sociological apercus you confuse reflection on facts with normative reflection. That Schoenberg is misunderstood today must be conceded; that the general state of mind that is producing this misunderstanding is questionable seems obvious to you: how then can you take up the pretensions of that state of mind as a norm and turn against Schoenberg without asking whether the Untimely One is not the Timely One from the standpoint of truth itself, and that accordingly it is these times that are untimely? This is a standpoint that you sidestep via a belief in the existent, which recommends itself but does not justify itself; you sidestep into the twilight of the concept of timeliness itself, which is ultimately good for nothing but blurring the severe compulsiveness of adjudication into the wait-and-see attitude of run-of-the-mill cultural-critical bloviation.

And so the captatio benevolentiae of banishing the artist Schoenberg into the realm of ethics likewise remains helpless. If he were nothing other than a 'venerable apostle of intellectual liberty' bearing a false message, he would be nothing better than an apostle of something only slightly less bad than monomania: the nonsensicality of this is so glaringly obvious that you could never assert it and cling to a reverential attitude that strikes me as more 'blasphemous' than any espousal of Schoenberg's work as a religious creed as long as this work is being registered so lukewarmly even by theoreticians of your calibre. If you wish to disparage this espousal as that of mere 'initiates' among whom you say I gladly and publicly figure, the fault here lies not in the initiates themselves but rather in that 'peacefully, quietly deliberative research' that certainly enjoyed enough peace and quiet to write the history of school choirs, and indeed, in its own terminology, to do so 'exhaustively', but not enough substantiality to utter any opinion on Schoenberg that was not actuated by sheer stupidity or by a kind of devious and cowardly sovereignty that thoroughly and dispassionately surveys all the possibilities at its command for the sole sake of not opting decisively for any of them. But the initiates are no esoteric coterie with initiation rites and other paraphernalia of the elect but simply a handful of musicians who share certain objectively grounded convictions, musicians whose circle has admittedly yet to be penetrated by even the most progressive scholars like Kurth and Schenker,[2] let alone by the functionaries of official music history. But it seems to me as if intellectual liberty is being sublated in a better way by these supposedly unliberated composers—by Berg, Webern and Krenek—than by those of their objective advocates who exercise their liberty of judgement mostly in order to betray the liberty that is the objective essence of their clients' case. Certainly you are right: Liberty may constitute the innermost substance of Schoenberg's work, but not as an abstract moral liberty but rather as the concrete liberty in artistic fulfilment—the liberty to be untimely in order to achieve what it is time to achieve. Perhaps there is an abyss between Schoenberg and 'everything that is known as youth', but not between what youth is and what remains mindful of the enigmatic interlocking of liberty and necessity whose ciphers are contained in Schoenberg's work.

Ever-sincerely yours,
Theodor Wiesengrund-Adorno.

November 1934

---

2 Ernst Kurth (1886–1946): Austro-Swiss music theorist; Heinrich Schenker (1868–1935): Austrian music theorist. [Trans.]

BRAHMS' PRESENT IMPORTANCE

The Lexicon of New Music (1926),[1] which takes it upon itself to apply present-day criteria to an appraisal of the inventory of modern music in conjunction with that of the recent past, says of Brahms, 'For the "moderns" he is undoubtedly the least influential of all the masters, which does not derogate from his greatness, the fulfilment of his historical mission, in the slightest.' The logic of this statement, a statement promulgated with that frolicsome enthusiasm for novelty that is ultimately inclined to jilt the new in favour of what in truth is utterly hackneyed provided that it is being passed off as something even newer, testifies against itself: for what could the 'fulfilment of the historical mission' of someone who has been dead for scarcely more than thirty years possibly signify if at the same time it is maintained that he no longer exerts any 'influence'? Despite this the statement is worth the trouble of a matter-of-fact rebuttal: not on behalf of Brahms, who is in no need of any sort of defence, but rather for the sake of substantive new music, which is misinterpreted and discredited by such theses and stands vindicated in direct

---

'Brahms aktuell' (1934) in *Gesammelte Schriften*, 'Band 18: Musikalische Schriften V'.

1 *Das Neue Musiklexicon*, Alfred Einstein's translation of *A Dictionary of Music and Musicians*, edited by A. Eaglefield Hull and published in 1924 by J. M. Dent & Sons. [Trans.]

proportion to its actual distance from that hastiness which in this case even more glaringly evinces the superficiality of the present than a lack of gratitude to the past.

First of all, even a *historical* conspectus of the origin of the new music precludes the vindication of this thesis. Reger, who this same lexicon generously assures us was 'the authentic historical link between post-classicism and post-Romanticism and the new music' is simply unthinkable in the absence of Brahms: his resumption of composing absolute music within the context of sonata-form works for chamber ensembles, his piano writing 'by touch', but even more profoundly his technique of breaking down unified themes into motifs, of shaping their metamorphosis through the application of the universally sovereign principle of development, and above all his style of *harmonic* polyphony, is unimaginable without Brahms; even Reger's most radical legacy, the composition of musical 'prose' through metrical relaxation, is indebted to Brahms' elongations and abbreviations. The extent of the young Schoenberg's debt to him may even be gathered from a superficial inspection of the song 'Am Wegrand' [At the Wayside] from op. 6—in other words, from a period in which his music was already evolving. It is less widely known that the early (pre-op. 10) chamber works of Hindemith also explicitly engage with Brahms. This ought to suffice from a historical point of view; all the same, historians could still alight on the bright idea that Brahms has been 'superseded'. So how tenable is that idea?

To be sure, nobody writes ponderous sixths over postpositional triplet grace notes any more; there are few genuine note-for-note repeats, even in the shortest piano pieces, and one can discern mimicry of the Brahmsian 'tone'—the laboriously loosened tight-lipped bearing, the wheezy respiration of a form of music that is, so to speak, relentlessly ageing—whenever one cares to look for it; this precisely because this tone is so intimately bound up with Brahms' origins—in other words his entire method of composition. But this tells us no more about Brahms than what 'every ass can hear',[2] to employ one of his own expressions.

The actual essence of Brahms is not so readily discernible; and yet in a latent fashion it is all the more powerful. It is most easily brought to light by a consideration of the material Brahms had to work with at the beginning. This was the material provided by Schumann—that melodic homophony that for the sake of song and its harmonic treasure trove had macerated Beethoven's great sonata-form edifice by steeping it in subjective expression, that had transformed that edifice's contrasts into lyrical dramaturgy, its tectonic repetitions into the compulsorily cyclical reiteration of the hermetically isolated ego.

After Schumann's sacrifice the objective spirit of the sonata recollects itself, so to speak, in Brahms. His greatness consists entirely in how rigorously this self-recollection attaches itself to the place and time in which it occurs. Immediate recourse to Beethoven in the name of Schumannian subjectivity and its related musical material is impossible; in the realm of sonata form, modern German and Chopinian chromaticism, which has not yet discovered from the theatre its major success in the mature Wagner, seems for the

---

2 An allusion to Brahms' rejoinder to those who observed a strong resemblance between the main theme of the finale of his First Symphony and that of the finale of Beethoven's Ninth: 'Any ass can see that.' [Trans.]

time being to be tantamount merely to an aggravation of Schumann's situation. Brahms' solution to this problem is not to blast his way through the material, but nor is it to turn back, at least no more than occasionally, but rather to *immerse* himself in it. His music gazes intently at its material, that very same Schumannian high Romanticism, in its self-givenness, until at length that material's own demands bring to term an objectification: the objectification of the subjective. That which dynamic tempestuousness accomplishes in Wagner's music is accomplished by dogged insistency in Brahms'. But Brahms' results have all the more staying power, staying power for the practice of later composers in particular, the less tightly they cling to the superficies of the sonic phenomenon and the less vulnerable to losing their potency as 'stimuli' they accordingly are.

A precise analysis of these results would be a major contribution to the theory of art—certainly no slighter a contribution to it than an analysis of Bruckner's. Here it is only possible to supply the following main points of the analysis: in Brahms' music Schumann's harmonic treasures are released from their expressive isolation, and the harmonic structure is redefined in accordance with them; they form autonomous subordinate scale degrees that make possible the meaningful chordal distribution of equilibrium even over long stretches and nevertheless pit their subjectively acquired abundance against the 'classical' schema of subdominant, dominant and tonic. Beethoven's lapidary symphonic style with its sequential treatment of motifs whose identities are consistently preserved (as in the first movement of the Fifth) is as poorly compatible with such a harmonic consciousness as is the Wagnerian chromatic sequence: in lieu of this, Beethoven's specific technique of development is improved and elevated to an art of variation, which in the exposition and

125

development sections generates the relentlessly new out of the familiar, the tried and tested, without granting admittance to a single 'free' note whose relationship to the construction is merely contingent. This is complemented by an art of economical dissection of themes into their smallest motifs, an art that logically develops out of the sonata much as Wagner's technique develops out of the compulsion exerted by dramatically pregnant characterization, yet without sacrificing the shaping theme as a vehicle of substance mediating between the motif and the overarching form. It is a grandiose, uncomfortable compositional *unnaivety* that is falling due only now, in today's illuminated consciousness of the material, an unnaivety that Brahms, in decisive contrast to Bruckner, keeps under masterly control and whose peculiar musical character as *knowledge* is giving proof of his curative power only now that the dolorous emotional urgency of Romanticism has died off. His idea of recasting and reconstructing sonata form itself has yet to be adequately tackled: this idea is formulated most precisely in the incomparable first movement of Brahms' Fourth Symphony.

But the situation of present-day music and the history of the problems confronting that music's best exponents make it impossible to refuse to give fresh consideration to those intentions of Brahms. Now that our dissonances are no longer of use as stimuli or as expressions of a chaotic spiritual condition, but rather simply as new musical *subject matter*; now that our recourse to neoclassicism has turned out to be too brusque, to be alien to the material, those categories of musical consciousness that Brahms developed out of the material, categories that remain undiscovered to this day, are falling due, are transcending that very material. Brahms' way of thinking about scale degrees is providing the foundation of all legitimate serial composition, his secretively inflective dynamics are becoming a corrective to counterfeit terraced rigidity; the economics of his art of variation perforce inculcates the economics of a mode of composition that is commensurate with the material; and let it be emphatically repeated that the reorganization of the overarching musical form that is commanded in Brahms' best works has yet to be achieved. It may easily even happen that the substance of the new music will be found precisely in the fulfilment of those Brahmsian postulates—postulates that may be analogous to certain theories of Hölderlin's late period—as the disquieting sounds secure their self-evidence as mere albeit undoubtedly necessary accidents.

Suppose the Brahmsian tone never exerts any 'influence'; what does such overt influence really count for in art anyway? He has instituted *laws* for art, laws whose binding precision vies for pride of place with their expectant clandestineness. At future Brahms performances that actualize these laws rather than his academic legacy or his autumnal colours, it will be significantly opportune to lay bare the laws and thus lay bare how fruitful they have hitherto been.

1934

SCHOENBERG

SONGS AND PIANO PIECES

The collection of songs comprised by his op. 6[1] is probably the work in which Schoenberg's music awakens to consciousness of itself. Its songs are singable by anyone who can master Strauss or Reger; its accompaniment is somewhat pianistically demanding, but the language it speaks is by no means unintelligible. One song is called 'Traumleben' [Dream-Life]: its melody, a torrid arc, stretches upward and downward in minor ninths above a foundation of irreproachably honest 'tonal' chords. Once one has listened to these ninths intently until they are no longer 'leaps' but rather properly melodic intervals, one has already mastered the first difficult skill one must apply to Schoenberg's later music, namely, an understanding of melody; for these wide intervals are dynamically *meaningful* and delineate this melody's shape. The song oscillates between E major and F major, but this oscillation is no impressionistic combination of oscillation and sonic interpenetration; rather, the shopworn ('Neapolitan') sixth chord of the second scale-degree, the ostensible F major chord, is elevated to a Neapolitan secondary key, welded to the key of E major; it is rendered so self-sufficient that it threatens to explode the tonal equilibrium.

'Schönberg: Lieder und Klavierstücke' (1934) in *Gesammelte Schriften*, 'Band 18: Musikalische Schriften V'.

1 Eight Songs for soprano and piano (1905). [Trans.]

And yet key is treated no differently in the later Chamber Symphony, op. 9; and yet again, in 'Traumleben', the exhaustive shaping of all twelve semitones into form-shaping scale degrees, which is the veritable fundamental principle of the much-maligned twelve-tone technique, has already been put into practice. Or consider a 'Mädchenlied' [Girl's Song] whose jagged, unprecedentedly plastic thematic work already resembles that of the First String Quartet, op. 7; its accompaniment possesses all the figurative wealth of a string texture. Or 'Ghasel' [Ghazal], a setting of a poem by Gottfried Keller: here, at the turn of the century, in the heart of the key of F major, Schoenberg is already absorbing principal elements of *fugue form*—a contrapuntally treated theme, augmentation and stretto—into the Lied and providing a model for his later fusion of lyrically melodic homophony (a homophony characteristic of the Lied as well as of the sonata) with the contrapuntal self-sufficiency of thematic 'development'. Finally and above all, there is 'Lockung' [Enticement], the masterpiece of the group: eight introductory measures present not a continuous unfolding of motifs (as in a Wolf song of the same period) but rather three quite mutually distinct 'figures', figures that are, to be sure, mutually related but that also sharply contrast with one another and give chase to one another in succession. One has only to play these measures over and over again until one hears them with their caesuras, their alternating rhythms, their tightening at the end, as a *unity*, as a 'theme', and the weightiest obstacle to an appreciation of the mature Schoenberg is removed, as one realizes that this disintegrated music is not decaying into its constituent particles, but that rather these selfsame particles in their irregularity are precipitately coalescing into musical *ideas* like the long and brief sentences and words of a language. At the same time the song is a prototype of those later anxiety-ridden visions that chase through Schoenberg's landscape until they petrify into crystalline repose. But the works that shine most resplendently in the light of op. 6 are the three evolutionary chamber compositions—the first two string quartets and the Chamber Symphony.

Similar floodlight-strength illuminative energies are contained in the fifteen George Lieder, op. 15. They are already 'atonal', meaning that they must be understood in relation to the structure of their consistently 'dissonant' individual chords and can no longer or only rarely be understood in relation to the diatonic scale degrees; but they still present the outlines of the traditional Lied forms and have recurring melodies, separate stanzas and a comprehensible surface structure. The accompaniment is in a certain sense *easy* inasmuch as it is accompanying a critique of musical language that pares away everything ornamental, every trace of cliche and convention, and merely sketches the bare outline of the object. The melodies are singable; from this one must learn to appreciate the independence of the melodic line from the harmony of the accompaniment, of which it does not repeat a single note because rather than drawing on that harmony it is added to it as a harmony-*shaping* element. The concision of these songs' expressive power is striking; striking, too, here—as in all of Schoenberg's works as heard by today's listeners—is the seamlessness of their continuation and development of the tradition of the great German composers, of Viennese classicism in particular—in this case, as exemplified by Schubert's *Winterreise*. The George Lieder furnish the missing link between the [Three] Piano Pieces, op. 11, and the difficult [Five] Pieces for Orchestra, op. 16 (a portion of which have been most instructively arranged for two pianos by Anton Webern); they already evince the free and yet very tightly controlled variation technique of the later 'rows'. From them it is no great distance to the works that are 'expressionistic' in a strict sense—to the monodrama *Erwartung*, to the music-accompanied drama, *Die glückliche Hand*, a work which, with its tremendous music of the smithy, its coloristic crescendo and its whispered choral passages, is perhaps the boldest and most inspired production of Schoenberg's hand.

There is a return to ease in the [Six] Little Piano Pieces, op. 19, a volatile afterimage of the great infernal compositions; they are tenebrous, wan, aphoristic—anxiety-ridden and liberated, just like the dreams of the morning; these could easily be the key to the preceding dark works, a key that is fully accessible to anyone already well acquainted with the George Lieder. Their crepuscular palette expansively shades into the motley gamesomeness of *Pierrot Lunaire*, his first reconciled piece, and at the same time the most seductive one he has yet written.

Next, after his long pause in creative activity, comes the twelve-tone music. The best introduction to this music is perhaps the [Five] Piano Pieces, op. 23, in particular the first one—a tender three-part invention based on a single row, a piece that also affords insights into Schoenberg's counterpoint in a keyboard setting—and the last one, a steel waltz that radically and illuminatingly presents twelve-tone technique as a new means of developing forms, an alternative to the means offered by the melted-down ruins of tonality. This set makes an immediate impression as music and is transparently comprehensible as a construction. Anyone who has an understanding of it at his command will not be nonplussed by the puzzles contained in the mighty late works that follow it.

1934

STRICTURES ON SIBELIUS

To anyone who grew up in the German or Austrian musical sphere Sibelius' name doesn't mean much. If such a person doesn't confuse him geographically with Sinding or phonetically with Delius, he is aware of him as the composer of the *Valse triste*, a harmless salon piece; or at the concert hall he has had one-off encounters with such program-fillers as *The Oceanides* and *The Swan of Tuonela*— fairly brief, rather physiognomically vague pieces of program music about which it is difficult to recollect anything.

If one comes to England or even to America, his name begins to swell to inordinate proportions. It is mentioned as often as that of a make of car. Radios and concerts reverberate with Finnish notes. Toscanini's programs find room for Sibelius. In lengthy articles larded with musical illustrations he is extolled as the most significant composer of the present, as an authentic symphonist, as a timelessly unmodern master and even as a kind of Beethoven. There is a Sibelius Society that nurtures his fame and busily furnishes the man with gramophone recordings of his oeuvre.

One becomes curious and listens to a few of the principal works—say, the Fourth and Fifth Symphonies. One studies the

---

'Glosse über Sibelius' (1938) in *Gesammelte Schriften*, 'Band 17: Musikalische Schriften IV'.

scores beforehand. They look paltry and Boeotian, and one muses that their secret can be revealed only via the corporeal act of hearing. But the sound doesn't change the picture in the slightest.

This is what that picture looks like: the things that are deployed as 'themes' are random sequences that are trivial and utterly lacking in plasticity; for the most part they are not even fully harmonized but rather presented in unison with pedal points, static harmonies and whatever else the five lines of the staff yield to a composer trying to avoid a logical chord progression. Quite early on these sequences suffer an accident rather like the one suffered by a baby when it falls from the table and injures its spine. They can't walk properly. They get stuck. At an unforeseen point the rhythmic movement breaks off: the progression becomes unintelligible. Then the simple sequences return, displaced and distorted, without making any headway at all. In the eyes of his apologists, these episodes are downright Beethovenian: they fashion a world out of the insignificant, out of the null and void. But this world is worthy of the one in which we live: it is at the same time raw and mysterious, shopworn and riddled with contradiction, familiar and impenetrable. Again the apologists say that this attests to the incommensurability of the form-fashioning Master, to his refusal to have any truck any with templates of any sort. But one cannot believe in incommensurable forms that are manifestly incapable of measuring out a passage in four-part harmony: one is inclined to believe not that he is superior to the established school in which he operates with schoolboyish material but merely that he doesn't know how to wield that material in conformity with the school's rules. His is the originality of shiftlessness; it is very much in the same vein as the originality of those amateurs who shy away from taking composition lessons for fear of losing their uniqueness, which itself is nothing but the disorganized residue of what came before them.

As a composer Sibelius is worth wasting as few words on as such amateurs. He may have garnered considerable glory for musically colonizing his homeland. It is easy to imagine that he returned there after his composition studies in Germany with justified feelings of inferiority, conscious as he doubtless was of the fact that he had not been vouchsafed the ability either to offer up a chorale or to write correct counterpoint; that he was burying himself in the land of a thousand lakes in order to remain safely hidden from the critical eyes of his schoolmasters. Probably nobody was more surprised than he was to discover that his failure was being interpreted as success, his incapacity as an obligation. In the end he probably believed it himself and then brooded for decades over his Eighth Symphony as though it were the Ninth.

The effect is of interest. How is it possible for such a composer to attain worldwide fame and classicality (however much that classicality may be the object of manipulation), a composer who has not merely been left completely behind by the technical standards of his time—for this is actually regarded as a virtue in him—but rather who is showing himself to be utterly inadequate by his own standards and making shaky and indeed downright bungling use of the traditional means from the level of basic building materials to that of large-scale construction? Sibelius' success is a symptom of a disturbance in the musical consciousness. The earthquake that found its expression in the dissonances of the great works of the new music has not spared minor old-fashioned music. This music has become cracked and lopsided. But in fleeing from the dissonances, people sought refuge in wrong triads. Stravinsky has exhausted the compositional possibilities of wrong triads. Via superimposed wrong notes he has demonstrated how wrong the right notes have become. In Sibelius' music the pure notes already sound wrong. He is a Stravinsky against his will. But he has less talent.

His devotees don't want to hear any of this. Their song hearkens to the refrain, 'It's all nature; it's all nature.' The great god Pan, with blood and soil in tow as needed, promptly makes an appearance. Triviality counts as originality, inarticulacy as the sound of insentient creation.

Categories of this sort elude criticism. That nature's mood is inextricably tied to reverential silence is their cardinal conviction. But if the concept of nature's mood should probably not go unchallenged even in reality, it most certainly should not go unchallenged in works of art. Symphonies are not a thousand lakes—not even when they are pitted with a thousand holes.

Music has cultivated a technical canon for the depiction of nature's moods—that of impressionism. In the wake of French painting of the nineteenth century, Debussy developed methods for capturing the expressiveness and the expressionlessness, the lighting and the shading, the bright and the fading hues of the visible world in sounds behind which the poetic word still lingers. These methods are alien to Sibelius. *Car nous voulons la Nuance encor*[1]— this sounds like mockery of his dull, stiff and haphazard orchestral

---

1 An allusion to Paul Verlaine's poem 'Art poétique' from the 1885 collection *Jadis et Naguère* [*Of Yore and of Late*]. The complete stanza of the poem in which these words occur may be rendered in English, 'For we desire ever more nuance! / No colour, nothing but nuance! / Oh! Nuance alone betroths / The dream to the dream and the flute to the horn!' [Trans.]

coloration. His is nothing like music en plein air. It disports itself in a rough-and-tumble schoolroom where during recess the youngsters prove how brilliant they are by emptying their inkwells. There is no palette: it's all just ink.

This is also turned into a virtue by his admirers. Nordic depth is assumed to be intimately involved with insentient nature and yet to refrain from frivolously enjoying her charms. This is an inhibited promiscuity in the darkness. Its asceticism of impotence is celebrated as creative self-discipline. When he has relations with nature they are purely internal. His kingdom is not of this world. It is the kingdom of the emotions. Once one has reached it, all one's further debts are cleared. If the content of the emotions is as little ascertainable as their basis in the musical events themselves, this is regarded as proof of their depth.

It is nothing of the kind. The emotions are ascertainable. Admittedly not in a way that might be appropriate to them; namely, in terms of their metaphysical and existential substance. They have as little of this as do Sibelius' scores. But they are ascertainable in terms of what triggers them in the scores. This is the configuration of the banal and the absurd. In isolation everything sounds workaday and familiar. The motifs are fragments of the lingua franca of tonality. One has heard them so often that one thinks one understands them. But they are combined into a meaningless nexus: it is as if nouns like *filling station*, *lunch*, *death*, *Greta* and *ploughshare* are being indiscriminately coupled with verbs and particles. An incomprehensible whole assembled out of the most trivial details produces a mirage of the unfathomable. One is delighted at being able to comprehend everything uninterruptedly and delighted with

a clear conscience as a result of the fact that one actually compre-
hends nothing. Or, rather: the complete lack of comprehension
that constitutes the signature of current musical consciousness finds
its ideology in the semblance of comprehensibility elicited by
Sibelius' vocables.

In the manifestations of resistance to progressive new music, in
the sneering detestation with which it is defamed, there resounds
not merely the traditional and general aversion to the new but
rather the specific intuition that the old means no longer suffice. It
is not as if they have been 'exhausted': mathematically speaking,
the diatonic chords certainly still afford countless new combinations.
But they have become specious and inauthentic: they serve only to
transfigure a world that is no longer transfigurable, and no music
that does not potentially carry forward the critical assault on the
existent down to its innermost cells of its technique has any right
to be written any longer. People are hoping to use Sibelius to evade
this intuition. This is the secret of his success. The absurdity that
the genuinely depraved means of traditional post-Romantic music
acquire in his work thanks to their inadequate management seems
to hoist that music out of its own decay. The possibility of composing
music that is fundamentally old-fashioned and yet entirely new:
that is the triumph that conformism is inaugurating under the aegis
of Sibelius. His success is equivalent to the yearning for the world
to be cured of its hardships and conflicts, for it to be 'renewed'
while still allowing one to hold onto what one already possesses.
What such fantasies of renewal as well as Sibelius' originality really
have to offer is nevertheless revealed by their meaninglessness. This
meaninglessness is not merely technical: it is no more merely so
than a sentence devoid of meaning is only 'technically' devoid of

meaning. It sounds absurd because the attempt to express something new with old and decayed means is itself absurd. Nothing whatsoever is expressed.

It is as if all the arguments that have characterized the reaction against musical cultural Bolshevism were finding their justification in this down-to-earth Finn. If reactionaries fancy that the new music owes its mode of existence to an insufficient command of the material of the old music, this insufficiency is nowhere more apparent than in Sibelius, who clings to the old. His music is in a certain sense the only 'subversive' music of our time. But not in the sense of the destruction of the bad status quo; rather, in that of the Calibanesque destruction of all the musical results of the mastery of nature that humankind purchased at a sufficiently dear price in keeping company with the equal-tempered scale. If Sibelius is good, then the perennial criteria of musical quality from Bach to Schoenberg—the criteria of evocativeness, of articulateness, of oneness in multifariousness, of diversity in unity—are now obsolete. All of this is betrayed by Sibelius to a nature that is no such thing but rather the shabby photography in one's parents' sitting room. He is self-interestedly contributing to the great attritional retail trade in art music even as he is being effortlessly outbidden as a seller by industrialized light music. But such destruction is masked as creation in his symphonies. Theirs is a dangerous influence.

1938

SCHOENBERG'S SECOND CHAMBER SYMPHONY

We are celebrating Schoenberg's eightieth birthday with a performance of a work that is still very seldom heard in Germany, his
Second Chamber Ceremony. I could scarcely imagine any work
better suited to this celebration. It unites qualities of the utmost
pellucidity with those specific, semi-occult structural qualities that
define Schoenberg's place in the secular hierarchy. Generally speaking, knowledge of the history of a great work of music's origins
affords little insight into the work itself. But even in this respect the
Second Chamber Symphony may be exceptional. Its moment of
conception dates back to almost fifty years ago; it was begun at the
same time as the First Chamber Symphony, and work on the two
scores overlapped. But the Second Chamber Symphony met the
fate of many of Schoenberg's other works in progress; it remained
unfinished, probably because the master's incredibly steep development by fits and starts in the decisive years just before the First
World War snatched him away from projects that were aware that
they were still closely bound to the traditional material of tonality.
All the same, by then the Second Chamber Symphony had already

---

'Einführung an die Zweite Kammmersymphonie von Schönberg' (1954) in
Gesammelte Schriften, 'Band 18: Musikalische Schriften V'.

reached quite an advanced stage of its composition. I recall that in 1925, Alban Berg, Schoenberg's pupil and my own teacher, told me of the wonders contained in its great E-flat-minor adagio, which he regarded as the most beautiful thing that Schoenberg had yet written. It redounds greatly to the credit of the conductor Fritz Stiedry, one of Schoenberg's most loyal friends, that he spurred him on to complete the work many years later in America. Stiedry subsequently also conducted the world premiere of the work at a concert given by the New Friends of Music in New York. His efforts converged with Schoenberg's inclination not only to revisit older, unfinished projects, as in the case of the *Gurrelieder*, but also and more generally to apply his latterly acquired sovereign mastery of new methods to old ones and to prove that from the perspective of the most progressive school of composition something new could be said even by means of those old methods.

The Second Chamber Symphony could scarcely be more unlike the First. Its overall tone is not fiery and tempestuous but tragic; from the outset it was conceived for performance by a small orchestra rather than by a group of soloists, and it was intended to consist of several movements rather than just one. In the course of its subsequent composition, its plan became more concentrated: the work was confined to two movements; although these contrast starkly with each other, they are tightly interconnected and together comprise a supremely self-contained whole.

We are dealing here with a construction in which the spontaneity and originality of Schoenberg's youth are united with the unsurpassed masterliness of his mature style. For the sake of the unity of the whole, the second movement was executed as a tonal piece like the first, but it is also suffused with a compositional artistry stored up by the entire experience of twelve-tone music; it is a tonal piece with a twelve-tone spirit, an integrated composition in which there is no longer a single contingent or non-thematic note and yet in which the immediate impulse of the composer as a practicing musician has not been compromised in the slightest. Listening to this second movement makes one feel as though tonality itself in its entirety were nothing but a special means of composing with twelve tones. But what makes the work unmistakably unique in the context of Schoenberg's total oeuvre is its unification of its technical construction with what may have formerly been called the poetic idea. No other of Schoenberg's instrumental works since his youth—apart, perhaps, from the Second String Quartet—realizes such a poetic idea so insistently. Only upon hearing the Second Chamber Symphony can one fully understand Schoenberg's superficially quite imperceptible yet unsurpassably profound love of Gustav Mahler, whose symphonies are similarly stratified as spiritual tonalities. The very technical modus operandi of the Second Chamber Symphony prescribes the path in which its expressive content comes to the fore.

The first movement is that famous E-flat-minor adagio, full of the noblest themes, but signalized above all by its harmonic wealth, that extraordinary abundance of scale-degrees that assigns to almost every note its own autonomous chord and hence its invariably participatory position in the work's overall structure and thereby achieves perspectival effects of the most extraordinary kind. In its basic character this movement is very highly yet restrainedly serious, lyrical and yet symphonic and expansive. The second movement offers a surprise. It starts in an extremely light, gracious, serenade-like tone initially reminiscent of Hugo Wolf. But thanks to the contrapuntal artistry that reigns supreme here in contrast to the prevailingly homophonic first movement, the symphonic knot is gradually drawn taut. The fabric keeps getting richer, more suffused with interrelations, and thanks to its tight construction it also keeps getting expressively darker, until this darkness explodes into full-blown tragedy and disembogues into a coda that harks back to the first movement, a coda that now elevates the lyrical sorrow of the beginning to a funereal monumentality. The second movement ends in the first, but it is as if it is only here that the emotional state from which the second emerged is at last being fully objectified.

Sometimes it almost seems to me as if the resistance Schoenberg is met with today no longer has any objective basis whatsoever but is rather merely a product of public opinion, which has accumulated so many cliches about his work that listeners now listen out for these cliches and no longer listen to the music. The Second Chamber Symphony is capable of enfranchising it from this fate. If you bring to mind the inner narrative that runs through the work and then abandon yourself to it without reflecting on it too much, you will be able to follow along effortlessly and immediately perceive everything that I have verbally imparted to you only so that your attention will be directed towards what is essential from the outset. You will be hearing nothing less than one of the richest, most beautiful and most concentrated pieces of symphonic music ever composed, and you will also come to trust that a man who knew how to say something so new by familiar means had the right to free himself from those means and in so doing yielded to a necessity that was even greater than the great tradition from which he derived his strength.

1954

Paul Bekker once remarked that the piano had been Beethoven's instrument of choice for his pioneering works. On the piano he first tested the compositional procedures and characters that he subsequently transferred to chamber ensembles and the orchestra. This observation is probably applicable to a much farther-reaching state of affairs. Throughout the entire history of later music it was the piano that composers felt most closely attached to, probably on account of the physical contact afforded by it, the immediate controllability of ideas conceived with the piano in mind. At the piano they followed their fancy in the absence of inhibition by elaborate apparatuses that were not immediately accessible to it, and yet in thereby saying what was as yet unsaid, they were not merely talking to themselves, so to speak. If Forkel's eyewitness account is to be believed, even Bach may have already behaved in this way at the clavichord. Chopin unquestionably behaved in this way, as did the young Schumann and the Brahms of the piano sonatas; and Schoenberg also falls within the scope of this tradition. Accordingly, each of the five sets of piano pieces that he wrote defines not merely a stage of his development but rather a specific type of composition of the new music, a type that invariably attached itself to that music. More fully than any of his other works, these sets in their

---

'Schönbergs Klaviermusik' (1961) in *Gesammelte Schriften*, 'Band 18: Musikalische Schriften V'.

unprecedentedness allow the listener to appreciate the necessity of those types. Precisely because every musical person can at least work them out on the piano without too much effort, they make for an especially good introduction to the new music.

The Three Piano Pieces, op. 11 (1908), are doubtless not the first atonal composition, as their opus number would lead one to suppose. At least a few of the George Lieder, op. 15, which were likewise written without key signatures and which no longer draw the customary distinction between consonance and dissonance, originated earlier, in 1907. Nevertheless, the Three Piano Pieces are rightly regarded as the beginning of the new music. In them something that is much more decisive than the admittedly interrelated phenomenon of the emancipation of harmony takes place: the emancipation of structure. By comparison with theirs, the compositional framework, the fabric, of the George Lieder is still conventional; they are the first of Schoenberg's compositions that dissolve the well-rounded, self-contained sonic facade. Contrasts like the one in the principal theme of the first piece, where in the absence of any transition a jerky passage in thirty-second notes attaches itself to a slow accompanied melody are absolutely unprecedented. The piece's vestiges of the ternary lied form are of scarcely any significance whatsoever when weighed against such innovations. Of equal importance is the simplicity of the second piece, the simplicity of a long adagio with two principal themes—a second simplicity. This simplicity consists in omission infinitely differentiated in expression via concealment. But the third piece is the prototype of a completely unfettered *musique informelle* purged of all memory of predetermined architecture, a music engrossed by a liberty of imagination held in check by nothing but the ear of the composer's inner listener, a liberty that even Schoenberg entrusted himself to only one more time, in the monodrama *Erwartung*. Even today the potential of this more than fifty-year-old piece remains unrealized.

The Six Little Piano Pieces, op. 19, are famous: their brevity, which was once shocking, has by the same token facilitated their reception. Expressionistic miniatures, they are most closely akin to those visions, those 'plaintive faces', which Schoenberg was painting during the same period and a few of which are reproduced in Josef Rufer's bibliography of Schoenberg.[1] The power of waywardness in them is extraordinary: a colour, a sound, gets stuck in place, refuses to allow itself to be wiped away and pushes the piece in its own direction; these are tears over which the visage has no control. Schoenberg's approach in op. 19 is closer than in any of his other works to that of Anton Webern, which was admittedly already formulated much earlier, in the penultimate song of Schoenberg's George Lieder. Nevertheless, even these expressionistic *moments musicaux* are not devoid of constructive traits: the rapid final part of the fourth is a rhythmic diminution and variation of the beginning that already quite strongly anticipates his treatment of tone-rows; as early as the continuation of the first piece after the rest in its second measure there is a retrograde (albeit not a note-for-note one) of the first motif, and the gossamer-thin last piece has been composed over a leading chord. The first piece ends compellingly as a result of the fact that the coda commences mezzo forte and unmistakably on the right beat for a change.

The *Five Piano Pieces*, op. 23, which originated after Schoenberg's seven-year creative pause, capture a felicitous moment: the moment

---

1 Josef Rufer, *Das Werk Arnold Schönbergs* (Bärenreiter: Kassel, 1959). [Adorno's editors' note]

when he is already working with rows, 'basic shapes', but has not yet committed himself to a count of twelve notes per row. Liberty and construction are rarely more perfectly integrated elsewhere in his work. The first piece is a three-part invention whose second theme, accompanied by a soft succession of chords, reshapes the long opening melody; the middle section and conclusion are then blended into each other. The brief second piece harks back to the scherzo form but rejuvenates it via the idea of having its vehement outbursts gradually die away until a reposeful line in the lowest register is left lingering, consolingly so to speak, at the end. The third piece, which has the heft of an adagio, is effectively a passacaglia over a five-note theme that enters solo like the first subject of a fugue; its brevity conditions each and every one of its closely interwoven yet sharply characterized variations. The repetition of a phrase from the beginning of the piece approximates the effect of a recapitulation. The fourth piece, on the other hand, is quite freely composed, prose-like after the manner of the third piece from op. 11; nevertheless, in outline it is by no means jagged but rather lyrically expansive and sweeping, like the exhalation of a single breath. The final piece, the waltz, is the first twelve-tone composition that Schoenberg ever published; it is based on the row spelt out by C-sharp, A, B, G, A-flat, F-sharp, A-sharp, D, E, E-flat, C and F. The ingenuousness with which the new approach unveils itself is almost awkward, in that everything that happens in the piece is derived directly from the original untransposed form of the row. Schoenberg was always capable of forgetting and re-forgetting what he knew how to do. In spite of the primitiveness of its row-technique this waltz is exceedingly rich in musical profiles. It is the first piece that makes renewed use of symmetries, rhythmic sequences.

The op. 25 Suite is the first fairly extensive work that from its first row to its last is fashioned out of a single twelve-tone row: E-F-G-D flat-G flat-E flat-A flat-D-B-C-A-B flat. The row is now also employed in inversion, retrograde and retrograde inversion. The expressive moment recedes in most of its movements. Four of them—the Gavotte, the Musette, the Minuet and the Gigue, are genuinely and unrecognizably derived from the treasury of old forms; the Gavotte is repeated note for note after the Musette, the Minuet after its trio, an elaborate canon in two voices. The entire work, as dazzling as a suite of steel furniture from the Bauhaus, approaches the contemporaneous phenomenon of neoclassicism from its opposite pole. Strikingly in evidence at the beginning of the Prelude is Schoenberg's directness, his immersion in the middle of things from the first note, the essence of his objectivity. Expressiveness returns in the Intermezzo, where constantly alternating melodic voices are accompanied by a ticking ostinato system; this accompaniment is interrupted by violent outbursts and moments of restrained lyricism. The Gigue, an exceedingly brilliant virtuoso piece, playfully out-Stravinskys Stravinsky in its rhythmic acrobatics but remains a fundamentally dynamic composition: distinct, self-sufficient figures of contrast are introduced into it. Throughout the Suite the rigidity of early twelve-tone technique is elevated to a process of stylization.

The Two Piano Pieces, op. 33, which have been presented to the public in faraway locales, finally show Schoenberg in sovereign possession of that technique. The rigidity has been softened; he moves about in the new medium with that casualness and liberty that yielded something like a second expressionist phase at the end of his life. But in both pieces the coherence of the autonomous form maintains its pre-eminence. The first is sonata-like in spirit, with two sharply dichotomous principal figures and a development-like middle section. After a general rest the recapitulation, the melodic resolution of the opening chord, is subjected so extensively to variation that it comes across less like a recapitulation than like a consequence of the momentum of the development. The second piece is songlike, cantabile in essence, distinctly ternary yet admittedly not without approaches to sonata-like dualism; a figure in six-eight time that also returns in the recapitulation approximates the second theme. The piece's exceptionally fluid mode of composition already points ahead to Schoenberg's much later piano concerto.

Else C. Kraus, to whom we owe this recording,[2] is one of those pianists who have unerringly recognized Schoenberg's quality and were interpreting his music long before he was banished to the unfashionable realm of the modern classics. She gave a complete performance of Schoenberg's piano works even before 1933, at the Frankfurt Music Studio. Listeners would be ill-advised to play all the cycles in uninterrupted succession. That could only cause confusion and the obliteration of that claim to the incommensurable staked by each and every one of the cycles. They would do better to play each cycle, and if possible each of the more difficult pieces within it, repeatedly until the musical experience has taken possession of them. This is especially worthwhile in the cases of No. 3 of op. 11, No. 4—and perhaps also No. 3—of op. 23, and the Intermezzo from the Suite, op. 25.

1961

---

2 See [Bärenreiter-Musicaphon Catalogue No.] BM 20 L 1503; the present essay was written as an introduction to this recording. [Adorno's note]

HARINGER AND SCHOENBERG

I have been familiar with the lyric poetry of Jakob Haringer, that mélange of Verlaine and infantilism to which Peter Härtling has dedicated his sensitive and beautiful essay,[1] since the early 1920s. But Haringer assuredly will not be forgotten thanks to the fact that Arnold Schoenberg composed three song-settings of poems by Haringer, including the one printed in this issue of *Der Monat*, 'Ist alles eins' [It's All the Same]. If I remember correctly, Haringer had also turned to him in search of financial assistance—surely not in vain. Admittedly Haringer's harsh fate did not fail to impinge on the songs as well. They originated in 1933, during the first few months of the Nazi regime, shortly before Schoenberg's emigration. Having completely forgotten about them amid the shock of the ordeal, he eventually stumbled upon them again in Los Angeles and then published them under an opus number that is much too high in the light of their chronological position in his body of work. To this day the songs have remained not very well known and are rarely sung. The last of them in particular is something of a

---

'Haringer und Schoenberg' (1962) in *Gesammelte Schriften*, 'Band 18: Musikalische Schriften V'.

1 Peter Härtling, 'Jakob Haringer: Hinweis auf einen Vergessen' [Notes on a Forgotten Figure], *Der Monat* 14(162) (March 1962): 52ff. [Adorno's note]

diamond solitaire in Schoenberg's corpus; a girl's song that is chansonesque in its intricate rhythms and richly woven piano part, perhaps in reminiscence of the as yet-unpublished pieces that Schoenberg wrote for Wolzogen's Buntes Theatre in his youth.[2] There must have been something of an elective affinity between Haringer and the man who worked the melody of 'O, du liebe Augustin' into the central work of his breakthrough period, the Second String Quartet. For the poet's sake as well as the composer's, one can but hope these songs attract the attention of the general public.

1962

---

2 These are the eight Brettllieder (cabaret songs) of 1901 that Schoenberg wrote as music director of the Buntes Theatre (Motley Theatre), the second Berlin cabaret venue founded by the writer and impresario Ernst von Wolzogen (1855–1934). [Trans.]

LETTER TO THE EDITORS OF
THE *LIPPISCHES VOLKSBLATT*
REGARDING BÉLA BARTÓK

In your article on Béla Bartók (in the *Lippisches Volksblatt* of 25 September 1965) I read that I had maintained that Bartók had been a mere imitator of the Liszt of the salon rhapsodies. I have never maintained anything so preposterous either in speech or in writing; rather, I have merely levelled criticism at certain structural compromises of a purely musical nature in Bartók's later work. Not only did I keep in close personal contact with him until his death; I also unwaveringly regarded him as a very significant figure. I was presumably one of the first people in Germany to recognize his stature; as early as 1921 or 1922 I wrote an enthusiastic article about his First Violin Sonata in Frankfurt's *Neue Blätter für Kunst und Literatur*.[1] And shortly before his death he even asked me to undertake an introduction to his Sixth String Quartet.[2] I attach the

---

'Zuschrift über Bartók' (1965) in *Gesammelte Schriften*, 'Band 18: Musikalische Schriften V'.

1 See 'Béla Bartók' in this collection. [Trans.]

2 This text, which according to a personal communication from Adorno was published in the *New York Times*, has not yet been located. [Adorno's editors' note]

greatest importance to having these things rectified and would be very grateful to you if you would publish a retraction of the misstatement. My esteem for Bartók as a composer and as a human being is most certainly no slighter than that which your article expresses with my wholehearted concurrence.

1965

KLEMPERER'S *DON GIOVANNI*

When a few years ago I asked Otto Klemperer to tell me frankly how Mahler had actually conducted, he replied on the basis of a crystal-clear recollection, 'Completely naturally'. What he meant by this can only be properly understood in terms of the specific value he attaches to naturalness: for him it does not consist in naivety and worshiping the great outdoors but rather in strictly refraining from shaping, brushing up or pepping up the music from the outside. He earnestly refuses to make the music interesting; he abandons himself unreservedly to whatever is unfolding in it. If the word *objectivity* [*Sachlichkeit*] had not become so toxic, it would be the perfect term for his ideal manner of performance. To be sure, in this version of objectivity no New Objectivist attitude simply steam-rolls over all musical expression and differentiation. But Klemperer does try to help the object itself in all its richness speak in such a way that it has no need of any additional ingredients.

'Klemperers »Don Giovanni«' (1967) in *Gesammelte Schriften*, 'Band 19: Musikalische Schriften VI'.

EMI 165–00 061/64. [Adorno's note]

This is the catalogue number of the original LP version of Otto Klemperer's recording of *Don Giovanni* with the New Philharmonia Orchestra and with Nicolai Ghiaurov in the title role. [Trans.]

In his recording of *Don Giovanni*, Klemperer comports himself like an old man reconstituting various experiences of his youth, and doing so with naturalness in the above-described sense. His approach and results prove to be uncommonly sophisticated. As a conductor he largely restricts himself to serving a supervisory function. In each number of the opera he establishes a kind of frame, a border that limits capriciousness. At the same time there are remnants of certain of his neoclassical proclivities of the 1920s such as an aversion to rubato. But the frame he has established affords the singers—and Klemperer conceives of *Don Giovanni* very much as a singer's opera—the freedom to develop. All musical direction from the podium is totally relaxed. This désinvolture on the part of the conductor stridently contrasts with the current tendency to keep a tight leash on every beat, every note, to refrain from loosening one's grip for even a single second. Only at the great caesura in the scene of the stone guest, does Klemperer intervene, in the true spirit of the baroque, and to admittedly overwhelmingly impressive effect. The tempi are also relaxed, serene, almost never hortative, but also devoid of the slightest trace of sentimentality. From time to time one might quarrel with these measured tempi; in *Don Giovanni* in particular there are certain alla breve passages that pose difficult questions about the choice of tempo from time to time. Nevertheless, even his rebarbative tempi have been chosen on the basis of accumulated experience; they are utterly uncorrupted by preciousness. On the other hand, whenever Klemperer does beat time more quickly in the manner made familiar by tradition, as in 'Là ci darem la mano', he makes it easier for the music to breathe and constructs quite unusual and compelling arcs of phrasing.

Although the whole maintains its supremacy over the parts, no violence is done to the latter. Whole and parts trustily vouch for the formal law of the work, the law of *opera assoluta*. In formal terms the opera presents itself as a structure composed of pieces, each of which bears its own highly particular stamp and stands out in relief from all the others in the aggregate, even as each of them, down to the level of its latent motivic interconnections, can in fact hail from nowhere but *Don Giovanni*, and such duality yields the only legitimate conception of style. But this conception emerges only in the specific content of *Don Giovanni*. For the equipoising of the individuation of the particular and the stylistic unity of the whole within this content is complemented by the comportment of the work's historical moments towards one another. Its hero— whom the skittish dramatis personae peremptorily denigrates as 'extremely licentious', as though the composer and librettist wished to apologize for centring the work on him—is the typical hero of the late feudal era, whom the bourgeois era he has stumbled into criminalizes, just as it criminalizes the figurine-like characters of the Marquis de Sade. Nevertheless, his antiquated libertinage simultaneously embodies the potential of liberty vis-à-vis the morality that is overtaking him. As the host of a party he invokes liberty by name even as he brazenly runs roughshod over other people's exercise of their own liberty. The opera serendipitously stands at the summit of the pass between the two eras. It is the tension between these eras, not what used to be called an idea, that actuates this theatre of the world. Klemperer's comportment submits to the ambiguous multifariousness of a structure that ought never to be forced into the confines of any overarching master concept. Moreover, there is a reason why this opera that gravitates towards seriousness of the gloomiest sort is called a *dramma giocoso*; among the bourgeoisie, Don Giovanni is not only a demon, but also, according to the rules of their game, a clown. The deeds of his phase of irresistibility belong in the opera of bygone days; just like Falstaff, he is no longer capable of bagging any new mistresses. Although he calls Leporello—who has a rough time under him and cannot break free of him—a buffoon, in this respect the servant is a mirror of his master.

The principal problem that every performance of this work must attempt to solve remains that of the relationship between the whole and its parts. Klemperer does not throttle the parts; nevertheless, it seems to me that they would require more encouragement than he grants them in order to come into their own, in order for this own of theirs to suffer no injury. There is no shortage of enchanting details like the unexpectedly cheeky whistles delivered by the flutes and bassoons in the catalogue aria. On the other hand, traces of asceticism subsist; often Mozart is shifted into the distance, as Bach tended to be back in the twenties. This is especially evident in the orchestral playing: it is as if the great conductor were employing his left hand all too sparingly rather than judiciously in shaping measures such as the two lyrical ones in the violins in the introduction to the peasants' chorus in the first act; one might also imagine Zerlina being allowed to segue more pliantly into the reprise of her first aria, and to sing it through less rigorously. Understatement preponderates.[1] Refinements must prove their mettle by not being emphasized in such a way that they are not emphasized. Ask only if they will not remain unnoticed as long as the interpretation does not thrust them into the spotlight, be it ever so discreetly.

---

1 *Understatement* is in English in the original. [Trans.]

It is also worthwhile to consider whether the delicate threadwork of the internal structure, its innumerable subtle contrasts, should not be more intensively worked out alongside the drastic contrasts of forte and piano—as, for example, in the quotation of *Figaro* in the banquet scene, a quotation whose two half-sentences are decidedly no less mutually distinct than fused together into a single period. Contemporary music-making, which had its first pioneer in Klemperer a full forty years ago, is beset on all sides by the difficultly of restoring to the individual details what was withdrawn from them in reaction to Romantic practice without thereby macerating the whole. Precisely for objective plenitude's sake, the overcoming of this difficulty entails an admixture of that so-called subjective type of interpretation that Klemperer renounces on many levels on account of his reverence for the object and by no means on account of a lack of vigour or imagination. The problem of the reparation of detail has become such a central problem of all music-making that no performer can be blamed for not having yet completely solved it. It remains to be seen whether it is completely solvable. Klemperer is most signally contributing to the solution by never treating the musical sound as an end in itself, by never once striving for a shining and sparkling play of instrumental colour and instead unperturbedly concentrating on what is actually happening in the music.

The work is sung by an international ensemble in Italian and in a highly Italianate manner, with fiery recitatives and a great deal of bel canto, in delightful contrast to the severe organization of the overall structure. The role of Don Giovanni is performed by Nicolai Ghiaurov. He wields his beautiful voice with great musicality and cultivation. The fact that he seems to be a bit lacking in suggestive power may actually be owing to the intrinsic difference between records and live theatre. On the other hand, in his recitatives he perhaps does a bit too much of a good thing with menacing laughter, which is really his substitute for a joie de vivre that is fishy in any case. Somebody should master the art of singing the breathless champagne aria in such a way as to let it out in a deluge while at the same time expressing its subtlest nuances.

Christa Ludwig as Elvira conquers the centre of the work by dint of pure musical quality. Thanks to her vocal artistry and express-ive articulation, this singer has become one of the most significant mezzo-sopranos available to contemporary musical theatre; over the last few years she has acquired a warmth that overflows and envelops the listener. The great arias 'Ah! mi dice mai' and 'Mi tradi quell'alma ingrata' are true pièces de résistance. If possible they are even surpassed by the andantino trio in A major in the second act, probably the most finished composition in the opera in virtue of its wealth of musical figures and perfectly balanced multifariousness, and in this recording it is thoroughly defined by Ms Ludwig. The role of Donna Anna is sung by Claire Watson. The level of expan-siveness and intensity that her soprano voice arduously manages to attain is admirable, but one cannot fail to notice that she is in danger of overexerting herself a bit, which danger is admittedly but the flipside of her intrinsically quite legitimate tendency not to be tied down to stereotypical notions about the role. Her voice is scarcely powerful enough for the grandly dramatic passages. Her coloratura lacks the sovereignty and security requisite to them, especially in the aria 'Non mi dire', with whose allegro section's notorious exigencies Ms Watson is not quite capable of coping. A coloratura singer in the grand manner must present what she has to give with a degree of facility and amplitude that seems to dash off neck-breaking runs playfully; when coloratura is merely up to par, it is already failing to keep pace with coloratura as an ideal. The double-sided character of the dramatic and coloratura soprano was self-evident in Mozart's time. Under present conditions it is scarcely reasonable to expect it—this is a historical limitation of any possible performance of *Don Giovanni*. Mirella Freni's Zerlina sings prettily and with great purity, although her singing does not contrast with that of the other women as malleably as would befit the role; for the sake of realizing the long-playing record as a form, the timbres of the various singers should be almost excessively distinct from one another, because of course it is these timbres alone that define the characters here. Mr Berry contrives to be a buffoonish Leporello without overacting so much as a jot. As Don Ottavio, Mr Gedda rises to the occasion with the quantity of good breeding that only that bridegroom's bridegroom is capable of mustering; Mr Monatarsolo portrays Masetto as a stage bumpkin in the old style; the great Commendatore is Franz Crass. They are all accompanied by London's New Philharmonia Orchestra. Klemperer's conception relegates the orchestra to a subsidiary function, which it willingly serves; understandably, the orchestra does not emanate much spontaneity. The instrumental basslines occasionally sound a bit lacklustre; acoustic conditions may be to blame for this.

It must not be forgotten that as a performance destined to be listened to on the gramophone, this one takes advantage of its exemption from all theatrical considerations by featuring very few cuts. If I am not mistaken, apart from a few genuinely dispensable secco recitatives, the only thing that is missing is Zerlina and Leporello's duet in the second act—presumably an insertion, as is suggested by the number it bears in the score. It would be instructive to compare the original Italian text with the standard German version, which instantly made the libretto unambiguously safe for middle-class consumption.

Klemperer retains the final scene, the one following the Don's descent into hell, owing to a neoclassical, and specifically Cocteauean, intellectual predilection for conventions that ultimately dates back to Nietzsche, to his hostility to Wagnerian music drama. Since then the notion of restoring the topos of the happy ending merely because it would be good to have one has ceased to be tenable. The grandeur of the Commendatore scene imperiously overshadows all the preceding dramatic action; anything that the restorative impulse allows to follow it cannot but be anticlimactic. No invocation of style as an authoritative criterion can exert any sway over a work that from atop its lofty pinnacle abrogates its own stylistic principle. The feebleness of the major-mode finale is no felicitous return to form: it attests to the extent to which Mozart has lost the power to bring the dix-huitième back to life. The finale ought to be omitted from all live, staged performances; to plead in its defence that it is essentially ironic is to undermine rather than to reinforce the case for retaining it. After all—if everything really boils down to the ominous criterion of fidelity to the original—Mozart himself had approved the cut before the premiere. The work must be protected from the incursions of a forced naivety, a naivety that the Commendatore scene—the last of the baroque allegories of premundane creation— retroactively damns as unregenerate silliness.

Anyone determined to listen to *Don Giovanni* with a fully attentive consciousness—to listen to it categorically, so to speak—will find Klemperer's discs inexhaustible.

1967

REFLECTIONS ON MUSIC CRITICISM

The very purpose of the event that we are privileged to be inaugurating in such an extraordinary setting obviously requires me to centre my remarks on problems in music criticism. The matter at hand might best be served if I don't strictly separate questions of theory and of praxis from one another. Even before I start I would like to ask Dr Kaiser, in whose presence I am especially delighted to be, to pardon me for making a few incursions into the territory to which his own lecture is devoted. Music criticism itself is of course two things in one, an activity that by its very nature belongs to theoretical consciousness but at the same time an activity that is practically invasive, often with significant consequences. My intention is not, for example, to develop for you a long-winded theory of music criticism out of an assortment of basic premises, a mode of thinking about which I harbour some very serious reservations on

---

'Reflexionen über Musikkritik' (1967) in *Gesammelte Schriften*, 'Band 19: Musikalische Schriften VI'.

Out of regard for his listeners, the author chose the form of a freely improvised talk for his inaugural address at the Symposium for Music Criticism on 12 October 1967 in Graz. Because he believes that the spoken and written word are not mutually convertible at will, in the present publication he has left it in that form and revised it only to the extent that he regarded this as absolutely necessary for its appearance in print. [Adorno's note]

philosophical and theoretical grounds above all others. I would much rather expatiate on some of the sensitive points of the problematics of music criticism.

I would like to begin by speaking about the possibility of music criticism in general, about the tasks that must be set for it and even about its proper object of attention; then I would like to say a few things about the necessary qualifications of a music critic before concluding with some comments on the critic's modus operandi.

First I would like to adduce the thesis that music criticism is not, as it often appears to be, a mere medium of communication; that it does not merely consist in passing judgements on impressions that one has formed and for some by no means transparent reason making these judgements accessible to the widest possible circle of people. Music criticism is, rather, when its concept is taken seriously—and this is undoubtedly true of every kind of criticism of works of art and of their presentation—a form in its own right, not a mere medium. In saying that music criticism is a form I must be understood as saying merely that it has an objective, material function and not merely a communicative one. In other words, if music criticism is to serve as anything more than a journalistic or didactic undertaking, it must in a certain sense be prompted by the demands of the music itself rather than merely by those of its recipients. The latter would be a travesty of music criticism, a caricature that is actually becoming such a widespread reality that a listener frequently learns how much he liked a performance from the review of it he reads the next morning. This surely cannot be the function of music criticism. Of the motives that are essential to this function and ought to actuate criticism, I would like to name only three without laying any claim to exhaustiveness. The first of these is the existence of works that stand in need of criticism. It is scarcely even possible—and I must ask you to forgive me for only asserting this thetically without grounding the thesis in specific examples—to doubt the notion that in an emphatic sense there can never be any such things as perfect works of art. I would unhesitatingly apply this thesis even to works that exact the highest demands and enjoy the greatest authority. In this assertion there lurks not an iota of disparagement of these works but rather a hint at a state of affairs intrinsic to art itself—the fact that it would like to utter, to capture, the absolute, but cannot utter it. Even as it is uttering it, it is losing it again at that selfsame instant. The prospective task of criticism is to determine the objective moment of the fallibility of those works without nit-pickingly finding fault with great, authentic works in the process. Given that it traces the inadequacies of works to their innermost structure, to their contradictoriness, it must to some extent rally to the works' defence, it must assist them even as it articulates the logic of their inadequacies, of their limitations. Works of art are essentially an intellectual phenomenon; they are works of art only insofar as their sensuousness is mediated as something intellectually determined and terminates in their intellectual content—in what may indeed justly be termed their truth content. This intellectual quality of works of art is not present in them once and for all; rather it is itself in constant motion, the same motion that every work of art already constitutes in and of itself. Works of art are themselves a process, and they unfold their essence in time. This essence is processual. The media of this unfolding of art are commentary and criticism. The significance of criticism for the unfolding of the works can best be clarified as follows: contrary to

a very widespread and persistent assumption, history does not automatically take care to establish the truth content of the works;
rather, the process via which the truth and untruth of the works of
art is wrested free of the bad contingency of public taste and historical preferences is situated in the foundational correlations offered
by criticism.

At this point, many of you, particularly those of you who are
disenchanted with current criticism, will voice the usual demurral
about the relativity of opinions about art in general and consequently
about the relativity of music criticism. Some very famous critics
who are significant in their own way have emphatically championed
this relativism in defiance of their own authority—for example, the
late English critic Ernest Newman, the author of a magnum opus
on Richard Wagner that has yet to be translated into German. All
the same, it is odd that despite his assertiveness he wrote concert
reviews for many successive decades of his very long life. I believe—
without wishing (and quite deliberately not wishing) to debate the
entire question of relativism in depth with you—I believe that this
relativism is illusory, an illusory assumption that criticism actually
terminates in the contingent judgement of the critic, that it is
bound fast to this contingency. Such an assumption is put paid to
by the critic's immersion in the aesthetic object, provided that he is
what I would like as undramatically as possible to term a loyal and
qualified critic. This has a direct and immediate consequence that
I, in accordance with the Hegelian philosophical tradition, regard
as the centre of criticism: that criticism that is compelling must not
bring to bear any sort of rigid, firm, fixed criteria. The task of criticism is first and foremost to detect new levels of form. This is not

particularly obvious. As a fairly naive young person, one approaches works of art with the tacit presupposition that each and every one of them is automatically striving for the utmost, the absolute. That is not the case. Innumerable works, including some highly illustrious ones, bear a moment of resignation within themselves from the outset to such an extent that they by no means impose the utmost emphatic demands even on themselves. Competent criticism will first and foremost have to address the task of giving an account of such levels of form if it does not wish, à la Stefan George, to make the Milky Way into butter, or, to apply a more trivial but more precise image, to shoot sparrows with cannons.

Some consideration must now be given to the itinerary to be pursued by such criticism. The first stage of this itinerary is the confrontation of artistic purposes—the confrontation of what a famous Austrian art historian, Alois Riegl, termed the will to artistic form [*Kunstwollen*], the will of an epoch and not of an individual work, with the means that are employed in the service of this will. This affords me an opportunity quite simply to emphasize that the talk about the relativity of aesthetic judgement is seldom seriously meant; that it is for the most part merely an excuse to dispense altogether with the effort of devoting serious attention to works of art, and that it is only interested in reinforcing the philistine's presumption that works of art are intellectual foodstuffs at best. The simplest version of music criticism is a form of instruction, of teaching. Everybody who has ever received music lessons will recall that provided his teacher understood a thing or two, in the course of these lessons he was taught the difference between a correct and an incorrect chorale setting, between a fingering that facilitates the playing of scales and one that does not do that, and other such things. In the course of putting these differences into practice, the pupil will naturally lock horns with his teacher in certain situations; he will articulate counterarguments, and as a result he may even do more than he has been instructed to do. He will consequently observe that when playing the piano it is sometimes appropriate even to linger over the black keys and so forth, but he will have a hard time doubting the legitimacy of his teacher's overall approach. What criticism in a higher sense signifies, and what allows it to proceed to address its intellectual tasks, is primarily its emancipation of such an approach, the approach of an intelligent and competent teacher, from the patterns, the tightly prescribed rules, to which one is committed by every form of instruction by the books, and its translation of its questions into the adequately purposive terms that self-evidently constitute the proper locus of immanent criticism.

I would never be so naive, and most certainly never so mendacious, as to regale you with the fiction that one can set to work practicing this immanent criticism more or less immediately. There is no critic or any person at all critically disposed towards works of art who does not apply his own experiences, views and even postulates to the works. Anybody who listened as a tabula rasa would presumably not be listening at all and hear nothing whatsoever; he would find himself in the situation that a Viennese psychologist has nicely encapsulated in the observation that to an ignoramus everything is new. Everyone is to some extent genetically compelled to bring to bear extraneous material on works of art. If this were not the case, no relationship between the aesthetically and intellectually discriminating subject and the object of discrimination could ever be established. It is therefore concretely exigent for the critic to learn on the one hand to incorporate what he brings to bear on the works into his experience of the works, but also and on the other hand to give an account of this incorporation and thereby seamlessly effect the transition between transcendent criticism and immanent, determinate criticism. To put this another way: in order to understand a work, in order to form any meaningful opinion about it, one must engage in a bit of make-believe. Anyone who cannot make believe at all about a work of art, who on hearing the first few measures of a piece of music cannot abandon himself to the eager sense of anticipation a child feels the moment the curtain rises, who is not then wondering what will happen next, and is not prepared to follow along even if the course of the work turns out to conflict with his expectations, will never be a competent critic. This very attitude of partial make-believe towards the work of art also contains a pre-emptive corrective to the usual superficial version of the notion of freedom towards the aesthetic object—a corrective that consists in granting the object the freedom simply to say to one what it wants to say. Accordingly, I hope that none of you just now suspected me of harbouring any attachment to the aesthetic of the 'authentic utterance'. Immanent criticism must also not be regarded as a spineless quest to determine what was intended in each work, for in intentional terms every work could be vindicated. I have had experiences of my own along these lines and perhaps I may be permitted to share one of them with you. I once voiced an extraordinarily negative opinion about a contemporary work, a piano sonata by Egk.[1] A man who is no great admirer of Egk but is generally averse to harsh opinions immediately offered the most astonishing arguments in favour of this sonata, when I believed I had quite conclusively shown why it was so bad, a mere decorative

---

1 German composer Werner Egk (1901–83). [Trans.]

trifle, or something of that sort; he said everything that occurred to him in its defence.

A work of art's right to special treatment as a work of art ends at the exact moment when it becomes evident that in such a constructed entity the means that it is employing are delivering a slap in the face to the task that it has set itself, however modest that task may be. Artworks' binding force attracts the attention of criticism not in virtue of its lack of a standpoint but rather as a result of the fact that its standpoint is sublated in a double sense, that it is absorbed into the object and vanishes in it. One might say that criticism is the paradoxical unity of a thoroughly passive, almost pliant abandonment to the object and the firmest resoluteness of judgement. For all that I would hardly deny that there is something like a shadow of relativism in critical judgement, especially in relation to very great phenomena—to Brahms, for example. It is necessary to pose the question whether notwithstanding the utmost adequacy of his means to his purpose, the purpose itself, meaning the objectification of an intellectual situation that I would like to term private inwardness, does not have something idiosyncratic, weak and inauthentic about it vis-à-vis the content of Beethoven's music. What may in an emphatic sense be dubbed the higher criticism, if I may poach this term from philology or historiography and transfer it to the domain of criticism, would broach these questions with precision and yet subsequently unfold their entire dialectics; it would in particular have to answer the question, specifically, of whether in art the accurate, adequate depiction of an intellectual state that may in itself be questionable is a worthier undertaking than attempting to depict a supposedly superior intellectual state in an epoch that no longer permits its depiction.

In saying this I am only indicating a problem, and I shall leave its elaboration to you. I am the last person to discourage the practicing of such a higher criticism, and I believe I have already made a small contribution to it. But at this point of all points I am not about to say to you, 'Don't be a coward.' Before the threshold that I have just been speaking of can be reached, dramatically objective distinctions must be drawn. In the first place, why Brahms, Schoenberg and Webern are great composers and why Sibelius and Pfitzner are bad ones is something that can be quite palpably demonstrated. Every self-respecting composition teacher ought to be able to demonstrate it if he is truly a master of his craft. However humble you may find this task that I have assigned to music criticism, the fulfilment of this task is initially adequate to the needs of the man in the street. To be sure, the telos of criticism, the goal to which it is orienting itself, is the truth content of works of art, and to this extent criticism is ultimately definable only in philosophical terms. But the truth content is not merely something signified by the works, something detachable from them, but rather something inseparable from their peculiar inner coherence while by no means dissolving completely into this coherence. It is not immediately graspable. The mediation of the truth content is the authentic locus of criticism. This mediation is essentially achieved via technical consistency. One must neither fetishize technique nor stoop to resorting to that empty expression *mere technique*. Here we are dealing with a third activity: the deciphering of the way in which the truth or falsehood of the structure of an object itself is manifested in problems of technical adequacy or inadequacy.

This is actually the archetype of the objective validity of criticism. There inheres in it that relationship to the object whose concept I originally somewhat dogmatically slung at you as something on the far side of the contingency of the judging subject. In connection with this, two moments must be distinguished: on the one hand the quasi-blind logic of the object itself, the compositional object, to which the critic must abandon himself; on the other hand the relation of this blind logic to the idea of that object, in other words, to that which is intended by the work in a higher, super-philological sense. Criticism must penetrate both of these moments. From this I would conclude that technical analysis is the sole site in which criticism is taking place nowadays, at least vis-à-vis contemporary music. Here innumerable questions are becoming decidable. Thus, for example, Alban Berg in his far too little-known essay on Schumann's 'Träumeri' illustrated the extraordinary multifariousness, the wealth of technological possibilities, inflexions and differentiations that inhere in this seemingly ultra-simple, ultra-popular piece, by way of imparting an understanding of why it may justly be regarded as a work of art of the first rank; whereas Pfitzner, against whom Berg polemized in those days, gainsaid such sound aesthetic reasoning and declared that the only appropriate response to the 'Träumerei' was to go into raptures about it; this was an approach that was profoundly alien to the very notion of art. Technical analysis, and it alone, leads to whatever transcends the technical. Perhaps I may be permitted to comment to you on an experience I had when I was a pupil of Alban Berg. He floored me with his extraordinarily harsh opinion of Richard Strauss; at the time I could not go that far, and even today my disapprobation of Strauss is somewhat more complicated and qualified than Berg's. But let us not dwell on that. Now the youngster that I was countered Berg's dismissal of Strauss by parroting to him a certain bit of nonsense that one imbibes as part of a bourgeois education and averring that surely he at least had to grant that Strauss' mastery of technique was beyond dispute. Whereupon Berg flew into an extraordinarily violent passion and said to me that precisely because in Strauss' music there was always something wrong with the innermost cells of the compositional structure, his mastery of technique in the higher sense had to be contested; that in this music there was absolutely no compositional coherence in a strict sense. At the time I did not raise the difficult issue that I became conscious of only later: that the very sublation of what is known as compositional logic in the traditional sense—compositional logic as originally represented by Brahms and still represented by Schoenberg—that the very sublation of this logic to a certain extent by the irrationalistic habitus of Strauss, a sublation that is ultimately quite closely bound up with the specific content of his music, is an authentic problem of higher criticism. But I would like to emphasize that there is something true about Berg's way of questioning. Over time I have learnt to give a wide berth to the expression 'but what about technique?' Technical problems and the question of the truth of a work's content cannot be outwardly separated from each other. Whatever is intellectually problematic about a work of art perforce manifests itself in the work's construction and in the latter's lack of consistency. Composition is in itself already a form of criticism; Brecht made an analogous remark about poetry. Anyone who understands anything about composition knows that a composer is incessantly having to decide between objectively right and wrong solutions, to be uninterruptedly mindful of antagonisms; in banal terms, he is always standing face-to-face with the question of the lesser of two evils. To this extent—and this may justify my thesis about its nature as a form—criticism is constitutively and by no means merely psycho-logically embedded in the act of composition itself. In this emphatic sense the criticism of a composition is the art or the capability of raising to the level of consciousness, of reflecting into consciousness, the immanent processes of composition, its immanent criticism of its own possibilities as it selects them. These processes—I am saying this only to protect myself from an obvious misunderstanding—do not constitute the entirety of a composition. Compositions also contain something different, namely, the moment of spontaneity. Moreover, if it is self-evidently necessary to be reflective in any meaningful form of criticism, it is likewise necessary not to withhold one's reflection from the other moments of composition; one must not cultishly adulate them any more than one would the so-called technical aspects. If objectivity in criticism is to be maintained, criticism must not be personalized; above all for objectivity's sake, if the critic is too short-winded and too short-sighted to immerse himself in the object, he must not have recourse to so-called per-sonality. I recently had an experience of this sort when during an oral examination I asked the candidate whether he was capable of stating clearly in objective terms why Bach is a much better composer than Telemann. The young gentleman—who, incidentally, I may assure you to your relief, passed the exam—couldn't think of any-thing to say in reply but that Bach was a correspondingly stronger, greater personality. Such a formula merely conceals the problem instead of solving it. The task of the critic begins precisely with per-ceiving the problematic character of one of these sorts of formulas, with specifying why Bach must be regarded as a greater composer than Telemann on the basis of his music instead of contenting oneself with observing that he is greater. The capacity for detecting problems when one's own overall consciousness is suffering from a false sense of security very much figures among the essential tasks of the critic.

Now let us turn to the question of the critical modus operandi. Today it is hardly useless to repeat a certain trivial truth. For present-day practice contradicts it in numerous respects. Criticism must pass judgement. Walter Benjamin once stated that one must choose a side in the conflict between schools and not worm one's way into the perspective of lofty objectivity aloof of the objective controversy, as Hegel put it, and stand above the object to be addressed only because one is not genuinely immersed in the object. The truth that criticism serves, that of truth unfolding in time—a truth of which I have already spoken—can be assisted only if the critic chooses a side in the conflicts of his specific time. The wrong judgement that for all its erroneousness still actually penetrates the substance of the work contributes infinitely more to the establishment of the work's truth than does that form of prudence that beats about the bush by adducing numerous scruples and reservations which for the most part are nothing but masks for calculation and cowardice. Perhaps one can give yet another turn to the argument by asserting that while it is certainly the task of the critic to disappear as a person into the object, he must apply the whole of his personal, subjective force to this disappearance. Moreover, aesthetic truth is not merely some residual determination that would be left over after the deletion of individual qualities. The requirement that I mentioned at the beginning, the requirement that music criticism should take the object itself as its starting point, additionally entails that in music criticism the criticism of composition should be granted pride of place. Such criticism, and first and foremost criticism of current compositional production, is the key. This means that in order to practice criticism, one must seriously know something about composition, and that one must not, in conformity with the general custom, merely pigeonhole the compositions from on high as instantiations of a particular style, or provide information about more or less superficial features of the compositions like their genesis, the history of their dissemination, and other such things. The task of the critic is to recognize the problems posed by every work of any stature and to proceed from considering the commensurateness of the means with its purpose to considering this purpose itself and the work's truth content. The principal criterion for judging musical reproduction is its degree of commensurateness with the object, and not, to be sure, merely with the notes and the expressive indications on the page but rather with the work's subcutaneous structure. The only sort of person who has any legitimate right to discuss musical performances is a person who in the first place can read music, and by reading music I mean reading it in an emphatic sense; but who is also capable of interpolating the structural elements from the score. No name or authority has any right to put him off from doing this. Thus, for example, even when his primary forms of reaction are vectored in such a direction—and it is probably scarcely possible for anyone to avoid this tendency—a critic must impenetrably and unyieldingly steel himself against such valid criteria as sensuous beauty and the seamlessness of the soundscape as soon as they start to count against the structural integrity of the object. One of the most embarrassingly conspicuous shortcomings of criticism is that precisely in virtue of being so heavily obliged to found its judgements on sensuous impressions it renders itself blind to such impressions. I recall once saying to my friend Rudof Kolisch apropos of a new cellist in his quartet that the latter's intonation was excruciatingly awful, and Kolisch replied: 'But don't you see? That's the best thing about him.' Now despite this the cellist was genuinely bad, but the impulse that Kolisch articulated is vectored precisely in the direction I am speaking of here.

In what I am saying to you here, I am trying to unite a certain kind of radicalism with presence of mind. For this reason I would like to impose a limitation on what I proposed regarding reproduction. Reproduction contains a moment that—how shall I put it?—is not entirely encompassed by the interpretation of the works. Ultimately of course in a certain sense reproduction is older; in a certain sense it is something antecedent to the production of music from its own point of view, something mimetic, something immediate. The interpreter, the performer, invariably has something like his own unique language. Anybody who as a child heard, for example, d'Albert play piano, heard Kreisler's violin, knows what it is about the object that fails to be encompassed by pure adequacy of interpretation. Criticism must also comprehensively embrace this moment. I shall take advantage of the opportunity afforded by this limitation to indicate a desideratum that is all too easily forgotten precisely in the theoretical register. Critical competence is the fulfilment of a moral obligation to take differentiation to its limit. A critic is worthy of his vocation only if he is able to recognize and comprehend the abovementioned mimetic quality of the performer as well as the question of objective commensurateness and moreover possesses the capacity to recognize properly the specific gravity of these moments in the result, in the performance as a whole. This renders the critic's task extraordinarily difficult. I said earlier that there is no such thing as a perfect work of art; it is even more likely that there are no such things as perfect critics. But it is still incumbent upon the critic to run his head against a brick wall rather than make a detour around the moments I have just described. Criticism also exacts a skill that the interpretive musician also stands in need of but that is rarely developed in music and that is seldom even paid any regard. The critic must be able to verbalize the specific musical experience, to put it in words that are not only commensurate with this experience but that also alight on the object itself. Anyone who lacks this aptitude, who does not have at his disposal a linguistic sensorium that helps him translate so-called purely musical processes into verbal concepts, and for the most part specifically technical ones, should keep his hands off criticism. I believe I am scarcely in any danger of being misunderstood to mean that critics should enrobe themselves in poorly understood musicological terminology by way of furnishing proof of their expertise. In saying that the critic must have a capacity for verbalization I mean that the specifically musical experience and the specific quality of the work must evince itself to him in a verbal form. This naturally also means that his description must not take on a life of its own at the expense of the object. Banausic criticism, which is incapable of giving utterance to musical experience, is Scylla; Charybdis is the journalistic type of criticism in which the description is an end in itself, an end in the pursuit of which the critic forgets to externalize his cognition of the object. The most important skill for a critic to have is probably an obvious one that on account of its obviousness tends not to be given any consideration whatsoever—namely, the capacity to have intellectual and musical experiences in general. If we take as our starting point a conclusion of the anthropologists that deserves rich credence today, the insight that the human individual's capacity for experience is dwindling, this capacity for experience is in reality anything but obvious. An endless amount of what is served up as criticism is actually only a surrogate phenomenon intended to conceal from the reader not only the fact that the critic does not really understand the object in a strict sense but also and more fundamentally the fact that he is no longer capable of primary experience and that, to employ a very common but very apt expression, he is surrounding himself with every possible thing extraneous to the object solely in order to distract people from it.

On the other hand, one must not be rigorously opposed in the wrong way to what is extraneous to the object. Music is not merely an aesthetic phenomenon; rather, it is always at the same time a social actuality. It is necessary for the critic to be incessantly reflecting on social actualities, on, for example, problems of present-day musical life; on the festival industry, the relationship between the repertory and stagione systems, the crisis of the soloist, and countless other moments of this kind. Kitsch, for example—and it is of course also incumbent upon a critic to call kitsch kitsch—is as much a social as an aesthetic category. But on the other hand, in brusque opposition to established practice in totalitarian countries, I would say that the social reference points of music must pass through the specific experience of music and that they must not remain stuck on its surface. It is not enough to subsume music from the outside under readymade social conceptions and evaluate it according to its degree of conformity with them. By no means should the social influence exerted by any work whatsoever be confused with its truth content. Criticism should try to get to the social truth and untruth

in the musical complexion itself, not cringingly defer to some exter-
nally imposed ukase that says that this must be and this must not
be. I myself made such an attempt when in its heyday I set about
exposing the pseudo-objectivity of so-called young people's folk
music, which of course is ultimately a social phenomenon, by point-
ing out precise compositional defects in such music.

Allow me just to list the key points of what I regard as the task
of criticism. It has got nothing to do with the impartment of
information in lieu of the disclosing of the substance of the object;
nothing to do with either literally or figuratively emptying out an
index-card file; nothing to do with any talk of genesis when what
really matters is, if one way may term it such, the result, i.e. the
work of art. Just as little to be desired are impressions or imagistic
manifestations of mood. Most of this happens in the absence of
any impression from the object. If the critic has first impressions,
he is permitted to share them; indeed, he is actually obliged to use
them as his starting point. But he is also obliged to carry them
further into the object and to acknowledge and correct the mis-
judgements to which everyone's first impressions are susceptible.
Today there is most certainly a danger that in conformity with a
great many other regressive phenomena criticism will dwindle into
to the type of writing that used to be termed music appreciation;
that the critics will fall into line with the prevailing positivism by
offering nothing but so-called actualities, facts. The threat posed by
such informative music appreciation seems to me to be much greater
than the one that may have may have been most prominent some
fifty years ago, that of the appearance of a so-called musical pope.

Now regarding qualification for being a music critic: I said that the first of these qualifications is proficiency at composition. It should be made clear that two traditionally avowed sources of such proficiency do not on their own guarantee it. The first is knowledge of official music history. It is certainly good and conducive to a dynamic understanding of music to be familiar with the historical interconnections; there is probably not even any such thing as criticism completely abstracted from history, because if there were it would be operating on the abovementioned fatal tabula rasa. But on the other hand with few exceptions the state of music history has diverged to such an extent from the intellectual content of the works as well as from their technical complexion, has deteriorated so far into both conformism and historical relativism, that for all the undoubted utility of historical knowledge, the science of musicology is tending to impede rather than fulfil the genuine desiderata of music criticism. There is a persistent tendency via the examination and certification of the alumni of musicology seminars to validate a kind of academic monopoly on music criticism; it is especially urgent at this time to be on guard against this tendency and to make sure it does not lead to the institutionalization of a sort of authorized Beckmesser-like pedantry.

But it must likewise be conceded that on its own a conservatory education does not offer the essential qualifications for the practice of music criticism. Out of motives about whose legitimacy or illegitimacy much could be said, conservatory training is orienting itself largely towards patterns, mediating general directives, and stopping short of addressing the specific qualities of the object, of addressing the formal law of an individual work. However good a thing it may be to have graduated from a conservatory or music academy, one mustn't believe that one is therefore eo ipso critically competent. The question of what a musician or intelligent person should actually do in order to qualify himself as a critic is getting me into a bit of a quandary. I cannot prescribe to you a sure path to the attainment of such qualification. It is certainly useful to have proved oneself within the context of musical praxis in some fashion, even if from the outset one has no intention of sticking with that praxis. The best course is probably to study with a genuine master, to become experienced as a composer in one's own right. To this suggestion it will immediately be objected that such experience puts one in danger of becoming partisan, of believing that only what is composed in accordance with the dictates of one's school is any good, and of rejecting everything else. I regard this danger as slighter than the one posed by the objective irrelevance of the critic who has not personally engaged with the genuine problems attending composition. Admittedly a critic must also be expected to be involved in a constant process of critical self-reflection; to be as little prone to absolutizing his own mode of reaction, in whose absence he can achieve nothing, as to yielding to any sort of external authority; and to be on his guard against resentment. To be sure, criticism must be defended against anti-intellectual prejudice. The sort of rancour against music criticism that is smouldering everywhere nowadays reached a flashpoint during the Third Reich, when Mr Goebbels abolished art criticism altogether and substituted for it something for which he invented the lovely label *art contemplation*. But on the other hand, the rancorous critic is as much of a living, breathing stock figure as the touring music appreciation instructor. And he is just as poorly suited to his vocation. Even more poorly suited to it is the musical diplomat, who is determined not to offend anyone. Instead of

moralizing at this point we should take cognizance of a problem—
a problem dealt with exemplarily by, for example, Balzac in his
portrayal of the typical journalist of the early nineteenth century in
Illusions perdues. A critic, and most especially a critic of any repute,
is always in danger of getting lost in innumerable entanglements
with musicians and musical praxis. It is very difficult to disentangle
oneself from these in the course of forming a judgement. I knew a
very famous literary critic who made a point of avoiding all contact
with writers. The results were not encouraging: he lost all contact
with the living movement of the object and ended up weeping and
wailing about anarchy a full fifty years ago. The critic who is not a
member of the inner circle, who does not engage in highly vital
discussion about artworks with artists, is isolated from the atmosphere that contributes so munificently to what I meant when I said
that criticism must approach the artwork in something like an attitude of make-believe. The critic must primarily have an affinity
with the most progressive consciousness; he must not, for example
try belatedly to line his own pockets as an expert on cultural treasures. It is a criterion of the true critic that he is capable of dispensing
watchwords instead of cautiously trotting along behind the vanguard
and sniffing out what questions are being asked. Legitimate criticism
must be to the fore of the works that it is criticizing, it must actually
discover works that it is capable of criticizing, and if it is productive
enough it will then most certainly find composers who are writing
such works. Moreover, it must not be cowed by the social interpenetration of institutions and customs or genuflect before them even
partly unconsciously. In a state of affairs wherein culture and chitchat
about cultural life have become to an extraordinarily eminent extent
substitutes for genuine satisfactions, and indeed, substitutes for the

substantiality of the cultural domain itself, criticism is in serious danger of merely doing its bit for the cultural gossip columns and drafting column-inches devoted to nothing more productive than such questions as whether Mr Richter or Mr Horowitz has lately turned out a superior or inferior rendition of Tchaikovsky's Piano Concerto.[2] In mere virtue of its medium, language, and its object, criticism is susceptible to being seduced into becoming the mere advertisement of upmarket cultural goods. Despite this it perforce entails a certain very specific kind of naivety, an uninterrupted love. Anyone who takes no joy in music must never become a critic; from the outset such a person is a philistine. Such being the case, the immanent moment of criticism also exacts a dash of amateurism. Those whose relationship to music is least amateurish, namely, composers, either have given the widest of berths to music criticism or, if, like Debussy, they have engaged in it, have found themselves overweeningly opposed to the moment of amateurism. The critic should sublimate his legitimate moment of amateurism via his experience of the object and yet the traces of his immediate love should not entirely vanish in the course of this sublimation, and he should avoid being transformed into a sullen specialist. But probably anybody whose vital substance is music is seldom still naively capable of such love. When a person has genuinely come to find music as life-sustaining as the very air he breathes, he can no longer be what is known as a music-lover. Accordingly there also inheres in the concept the critic something that is the opposite of what I have been describing to you. The critic must not be capable of nothing but love; he must also be acquainted with disgust. Criticism requires

---

2 Presumably his Piano Concerto No. 1 in B-flat minor, op. 23. [Trans.]

one to be strong enough to negate things. The critic must not only steel himself against cliches in music and cliches about music; he must also actively pit himself against them. He cannot get away with playing along. Anyone who is not critical in the sense of wanting things to be different than they are is worthless as a critic. The type of critic whom musicians despise for clinging to artists like a bedbug is surely the least qualified of all.

I only have enough time left to make a few remarks about the modus operandi of the critical mind. To the extent that this is at all practicable, it is advisable to study the scores, to acquire knowledge of the works themselves, even though there is nothing that more readily causes the connoisseur to become jaded. How best to proceed in individual cases, whether, for example, to study the score first and then surrender oneself to one's impression or vice-versa is something everyone must figure out for himself based on his own experience. To be sure, when one has not taken in a complete view of the object or listened to it all the way through, one must have the civil courage to admit this. This is a piece of critical morality. I have not spoken to you of this morality so far because every idea that I have articulated actually moves within the ether that could be described as critical morality. Anyone who is sure of himself must also say when he is unsure of himself. If at all possible one must avoid expressing mere judgements of taste. Whenever one does express them, although one obviously must act on the impulses supplied by one's taste, one must further transpose them into objectively grounded terms. One should never deliver pat, unfounded judgements, especially not in such a form that one imagines that one has thereby said the last word on an object, that one has subsumed it under its clinching umbrella-concept. I know, for example, regarding

Berg, of whom I have spoken at various times today, that innumerable critics believed that they were securing themselves a kind of pre-eminence in virtue of the fact that they were writing that he was really just a late Romantic, as if they had already achieved something with such a statement, or a statement that this is really just expressionism or really just such and such. One of the duties of critical self-reflection is the avoidance of judgements of the form X is Y. The most immoral act criticism can commit—an act that is nevertheless closely bound up with the present day's informational mischief-making, its propensity for sloganeering and headline-mongering—is probably to cast aspersions on an object or an artist without consequently offering any insight into the object itself. Equally problematic is the empty ostentation of erudition, the employment of strips and scraps of culture as a substitute for objective competence. Complementarily, the total and ruthless demolition of all cliche-ridden and reified ideas is one of the most important duties of criticism. If, in a manner analogous to that of Karl Kraus, a music critic were ever to carry out raids on terms like *born musician, elemental rhythmic power, late Romanticism,* or *intellectually refined*—one could compile an entire index of such coinages—a procession of verbal phantoms would form, a procession from which he would recoil in horror. Thus as a legitimate critic one must also take a stance against the stereotypical fame of epochs like the baroque and even against all glorification of individual works that is completely detached from their intrinsic quality. I myself once tried to do this in connection with the *Missa Solemnis*, not by belittling it but by simply showing how very deeply embedded the problem contained in this work is, how very poorly it is still generally understood, and how, such being the case, its fame is a mere chimera. That on its own was enough to raise people's hackles. Finally I would like to argue very strongly in favour of the reviewing of gramophone records, which today is still very much a sideline of official criticism. More attention to records would be of great value not only on account of their increasing significance in musical life, but also and above all because thanks to the repeated confrontation of the faculty of critical judgement with the object that is permitted by the record, criticism would thereby come much closer to its phenomenon than ever before. The ideal form of criticism, especially in the domain of the criticism of performances, would be one that could immediately point to musical examples. Somebody should try making use of a technique developed in radio, that of the *running commentary* of critical remarks on the phenomenon at the very moment it is unfolding.[3] If, for example, a conductor starts employing an unmotivatedly fast tempo merely for superficial effect, the critic should jump in and shout: 'Why is he playing faster? That's really inappropriate here,' or something similar. I have actually already tried doing this once, during a broadcast about Toscanini, and my intervention didn't exactly make me very popular. Above all I would like to ask you, in the event that many of the reflections that I have made sound only too reasonable to you, to bear in mind that it can be said of almost all the moments that I have highlighted here that if one seriously tries to put them into practice, they will be met with howls of resistance from even the most quiescent souls, which goes to show that the indurations and reifications against which they are directed are more powerful than we can even imagine. To be sure, the morality of criticism would be improved by the implementation

---

3 *Running commentary*: in English in the original, but Adorno writes *running comment*. [Trans.]

of my methods inasmuch as they would be subject to verification via reference to the phenomenon under consideration—in this case, gramophone records. In such situations the critic would really no longer be the demigod who he so cavalierly pretends to be; rather, he would be a discussion-participant in the most literal sense. I believe that it is the demigods above all others who would be bound to expose their own incompetence in such a discussion.

Accordingly there is really nothing left for me to say to you but that the task of the critic is to retranslate the musical work out of a congealed, indurated, ossified condition into the force-field that every such work and every performance actually is. That alone, and not the so-called temperament of the critic, is adequate to the concept of vital criticism.

1967

TELEVISED MUSIC IS A POINTLESS RIGMAROLE

AN INTERVIEW IN *DER SPIEGEL* (26 FEBRUARY 1968)

SPIEGEL. Professor Adorno, you once dismissed radio concerts as empty strumming and chirping. Does this characterization likewise apply to the performances of baroque concertos, classical symphonies, masses and operas that are ever more frequently available for hearing and viewing on the first and second television channels?[1] Is it possible to present an adequate performance of music on television?

ADORNO. As an optical medium, television is to a certain extent intrinsically alien to music, which is essentially acoustic. From the outset, the technology of television occasions a certain displacement of attention that is disadvantageous to music. In general music exists to be heard and not to be seen. Now one can certainly say that there are certain modern pieces in which the optical aspect also has a certain importance. But at least in the case of traditional music . . .

'Musik im Fernsehen ist Brimborium' (1968) in *Gesammelte Schriften*, 'Band 19: Musikalische Schriften VI'.

1 *The first and second television channels*: those of the Federal Republic of Germany's two nationwide public-broadcasting networks, ARD and ZDF. [Trans.]

SPIEGEL. . . . obviously on German television—aside from the third channels[2]—only traditional music is music is performed . . .

ADORNO. . . . in the case of traditional music there is something unseemly about the whole thing, an unseemliness naturally occasioned by the fact that by analogy with its counterpart in radio, a piece of machinery like the television-production process has got to be constantly fed, that something has got to be getting constantly stuffed into the sausage machine. On the whole I believe that the very act of performing music on television entails a certain displacement that is detrimental to musical concentration and the meaningful experience of music.

SPIEGEL. We don't believe that the receptive capacity of consumers of television is completely engrossed by the optical element. Don't you think that the medium of television can also be acoustically stimulating?

ADORNO. I by no means wish to deny that the medium of television can also be acoustically stimulating, or even that its optical procedures can have certain benefits for music. Perhaps I can clarify this with an example: my late teacher Alban Berg was always toying with the seemingly quite paradoxical idea of having *Wozzeck*, which really is one of the last operas in a strict sense, made into a film, not, to be sure, out of anything like a desire to break into the so-called mass-media—he had absolutely no interest in things like that—but because he believed that by filming the work one could make its musical events more malleable, so to speak, than is the case in normal opera performances.

---

2 *The third channels*: the television channels of the Federal Republic's regional broadcasting networks. [Trans.]

For example, through the techniques of the roving microphone, which of course correspond to the changing camera positions in the film, one could bring out the main voice at any given time more meaningfully, more malleably, than was possible in an ordinary opera performance in Berg's opinion.

SPIEGEL. Admittedly, such possibilities don't seem to be available in television. We've heard about thirty televised concerts and opera performances; for example, a performance of the Cappella Coloniensis in the Kaisersaal of Corvey Abbey, lots of baroque music, Handel, Purcell, Bach played on one, two and three organs by Professor Nowakowski; Beethoven symphonies, of course; Schubert's *Winterreise*, of course, sung by Hermann Prey, who additionally sang a potpourri of opera arias called 'Schaut her, ich bin's'.[3] There was also an *Arabella* and a colourful performance of *Figaro* by the Hamburg State Opera in which a great many shots were extremely embarrassing because the close-ups showed how grotesquely the singers had to contort their faces in order to preserve their impeccable intonation . . . On top of that the sound engineer cranked up the volume during the arias, as if he were trying to say, 'Now you've got your lovely melodies that are the only reason you're slogging through this whole opera.' Then during Verdi's *Requiem* conducted by Herbert von Karajan the camera evinced especial fondness for the maestro's closed eyes.

ADORNO. Your observations are quite correct, and I think we shall be of one mind about the conclusions to be drawn from them.

---

3 *Professor Nowakowski*: the German organist, conductor and composer Anton Nowakowski (1897–1969); *Schaut her, ich bin's*: 'Look Here, It's Me.' [Trans.]

SPIEGEL. Yes, if you can acknowledge that there is something second-rate about television productions of music—namely, the fact that the technical means, the execution, the craftsmanship involved, gains primacy over the music.

ADORNO. Yes, one's attention is drawn away from the essential things and towards the inessential ones, namely, away from the music as an end and towards the means, the manner, in which the keyboardists and wind players and string players are playing it. But I'd like to point out that these irritating practices are well established in the techniques of all forms of mechanical reproduction. In radio and in many gramophone recordings one also encounters a predilection for accentuating so-called principal voices or so-called melodies out of all proportion to their place in the musical fabric. This is the fault of the sound engineers, who subsequently engage in fundamentally quite unmusical procedures by surgically extracting these voices, which is quite in keeping with their—if I may say this—unartistic intuitions and is also congenial to the highly problematic taste of the public.

SPIEGEL. But thanks to their training, the sound engineers obviously should be capable of realizing the musical and aesthetic intentions of the conductors by technical means.

ADORNO. It's hard to say. On the one hand, they've got to yield to certain technological exigencies—by, for example, making sure that the dynamic levels are kept within the limits of what is possible in this medium. But on the other hand—I remember this in particular of the practices of the film studios as I became familiar with them in Hollywood—they're guided by their own intuitions. They determine what sounds good and what sounds bad to them, and they unreflectively adjust the recording in accordance with this determination. All the while, most of them are operating in conformity with completely obsolete musical conventions. What results from this is that certain middle-of-the-road so-called euphony, that culinary seasoning of the sound at the expense of all the structural elements of the music. This is of course partly owing to the fact that the engineers are practically all recruited from the ranks of technicians, because so far nobody has managed to bring in people who obviously aren't very easy to come by—people who are technically competent and at the same time genuinely musically talented and well-educated to boot. If this were changed, a lot of things would be better.

SPIEGEL. The culinary element seems to us to be especially prominent in music broadcasts. A candlelit Karajan and Menuhin concert framed by the plush furnishings of a Viennese salon; Bach passions and cantatas in the obvious setting, a baroque church. As the distinguished vocal soloist is singing his part . . .

ADORNO. . . . the listeners make furiously sorrowful faces . . .

SPIEGEL. . . . and the camera fondles lovably chubby-cheeked putti and Madonnas. Is this acceptable?

ADORNO. It's horrible, the worst sort of commercialization of art. Here the mass media—which precisely because they are technical media are duty-bound to forgo everything unseemly and gratuitous—are conforming to the abominable convention of showcasing lady harpsichordists with snail shell-braids over their ears who brainlessly and ineptly execute Mozart on jangly candlelit ancient keyboards. I think it's more than high time for purging the mass media of all this illusional kitsch and of the whole Salzburg phantasmagoria that's forever haunting it.

SPIEGEL. Are you really of the opinion that this kitsch engenders a completely distorted image of the music?

ADORNO. It engenders an absolutely inadmissible image, above all because here an illusional element also supervenes; it's as if one were present at some sort of shrine where a unique ritualistic event were being enacted in the *hic et nunc*—a notion that is completely incommensurable with the mass reproduction that causes this same event to be seen in millions of places on millions of television screens.

SPIEGEL. Television critics have taken umbrage at the fact that star conductors—and they're the only ones who appear on German television—have got to be fascinating at the drop of a hat. Is this actually an unwritten law of the mass media?

ADORNO. This reminds me of that charming anecdote about the two cultural hyenas who were sitting at a Nikisch concert maybe sixty years ago or even longer than that. The one lady pokes the other one and says, 'If he starts to get fascinating, please give me a poke.'[4] This completely gratuitous, manipulative concept of the fascinating conductor is an appalling nuisance. If musical life in general weren't so thoroughly dominated by false personalization, all of this would inevitably have long since vanished without a trace. If I may take the liberty of mentioning this, in the last chapter of my book *Der getreue Korrepetitor* [The Loyal

---

4 *Nikisch*: the Hungarian conductor Arthur Nikisch (1855–1922). [Trans.]

Répétiteur] I have tried to develop some thoughts on how to apply the medium of radio appropriately to music and even set forth a highly detailed programmatic description of how one would have to go about doing this. But I am afraid that precious little of this has seeped into anybody's consciousness through the cracks in official musical life.

SPIEGEL. Have the people in charge of the broadcasting networks really not been listening to you?

ADORNO. I can't say that my suggestions of an appropriate application of the so-called mass media—for example, of broadcasting music with a *running commentary*,[5] with an analytical commentary that runs in synchrony with the work—have yielded many practical results.

SPIEGEL. Are the proposals you've tendered for radio transferable to television? In other words, is there a specific form that's appropriate to the presentation of music on television?

ADORNO. This is the crux of the matter. What I mean is that they've been making do with something that's quite similar to the way things are done in, for example, the film business—with cannibalizing and peddling the cultural artefacts that are ready to hand, even when this flagrantly contradicts the character of the media, instead of developing specific new possibilities out of the medium itself. Of course there is an entire group of avant-garde artists who think differently; for example, Stockhausen has called for quite similar things independently of me. I'm

---

5 Here, as in 'Reflections on Music Criticism', Adorno writes *running comment*. [Trans.]

also thinking of the most recent attempts of Mauricio Kagel, which are absolutely tantamount to a meaningful application of television. But this is just a drop in the ocean compared with the dominant mode of production in the culture industry. Consequently, one can never shake the feeling that such things must be regarded as grudgingly doled-out servings of schmaltz within the politics of programming, wherein the so-called desires of the public, which I have absolutely no inclination to gainsay, are oftentimes employed as an ideological excuse for feeding the public mendacious rubbish and kitsch. I would also include in this kitsch the kitschified production styles applied to the presentation of so-called—I might have almost said *rightly* so-called—classic cultural artefacts.

SPIEGEL. Take for example Brahms' *German Requiem* on the second channel. The images concurrently broadcast with it were of trees, forests, lakes, fields, monuments and cemeteries.

ADORNO. The acme of wanton stupidity. It's just aping the standard use of nature sequences in commercial films.

SPIEGEL. Do you mean to imply that the people in charge of the television networks don't understand that this way of presenting music contributes to cultural stultification?

ADORNO. I'd like to answer your question in sociological terms. There's a certain dead weight of the apparatus that wins out, in a way that should be analysed at some point, against the better judgement and against the will of the people involved. The magazine the *New Yorker* once showed in an analysis how a film that's intended to be of decent quality and meaningful ends up being just another kitschy product exactly like all the others against the will of all the people involved simply on account of the awful apparatus, which has taken on a life of its own. I believe that an analysis of these objective processes would get us further than thinking about them in terms of incompetent individuals. Being involved in this whole sphere always entails being constantly confronted by so-called technological exigencies. The worst things are always underpinned by the best objective arguments. And so you very easily get a feeling of helplessness. The first thing that one would have to ask television to do in this regard is to get around to broaching the question of a televisually specific form of music or of a televisual way of relating to music and especially to opera, instead of producing all this falsehood and inadequacy, instead of simply making do with the sterile photographic duplication of such events.

SPIEGEL. So far you've only offered criticism. Can you tender any proposals for a televisually specific form of music? There have of course already been some rudimentary attempts at this. The Swiss composer Heinrich Sutermeister has written a television opera, and Benjamin Britten is working on one.

ADORNO. Quite often these are simply hybrid products, the products of an awkward situation. The composers need money, which God knows is nothing they should be blamed for, and so they get mixed up in such things without having had the freedom to think through the dramaturgical possibilities completely in the context of the industry in its present state. Whether there can be something like a form of music unique to television, in other words, music that's absolute and that at the same time intrinsically stands in need of a visual supplement, is something

I don't know. I must say that for the time being I have grave doubts about this, although I'm quite happy to be convinced that they're misplaced. Rudimentary attempts are indeed being made. Musicians like Stockhausen, like Kagel, like the highly talented György Ligeti, are occupying themselves quite seriously with these things.

SPIEGEL. That's true. But their efforts are shown behind virtually closed doors—in other words, on the third channels. On the first and second channels, on the other hand, one gets the standard cultural artefacts—for example, *Der Freischütz*—not once but twice—*Madama Butterfly*, the *Missa Solemnis* and *Eine Kleine Nachtmusik*. To judge by the selection, it's the culinary moment, the culture consumer-oriented moment, that's given pride of place.

ADORNO. Parenthetically, I believe that in this case something else is supervening in what you call the culinary element, something social. What's being savoured here is not only the pleasure of pure euphony but also prestige. From the outset such constructions are governed by the tacit premise that the pinnacles of cultural life are Salzburg or Bayreuth or the major festivals in Edinburgh or in Venice or wherever else. When this is served up onscreen, there's this sense that nothing is too lofty or expensive for us to present to you, the television viewer, and so you can participate in these events parasitically, in a manner of speaking. Latent in this is a profoundly conformist disposition to the dominant culture industry.

SPIEGEL. You just used the word *parasitic*. Is it really fair to call it that, since after all, the festivals can only be attended by a small number of people?

ADORNO. Yes, it's parasitic, but Lord knows when I said that I didn't mean to disparage the people who experience the festivals vicariously through television. But the truth is that there's no genuine contact between the performance and the audience in this case. It's entirely the fault of an apparatus that keeps reinforcing, redoubling, the prestige and the cultural prattle engendered by a high-intensity publicity machine. This gives rise to the mistaken impression that these star-studded performances—which do indeed often showcase some truly marvellous voices and colossally virtuosic conductors, but which are hardly ever truly artistically integrated—are the pinnacles of music and of culture in general. This culture is supposed to be democratic, but there is something inherently artificial, inherently ersatz, in this manipulation of democracy. It's a pseudodemocracy.

SPIEGEL. Let's return to the subject of the selection of repertoire. So the television viewer is allowed to consume the same cultural wares over and over again, to consume what is barbarously known as 'classical' music. As you yourself have put it, 'Whatever is most familiar is most successful.' And this viewer is always seeing the same conductors. Above all Karajan with his telegenic gestures.

ADORNO. He's being converted into an actor who performs an impersonation of his own artistic achievement.

SPIEGEL. And are you of the opinion that this no longer has anything to do with musical achievement and interpretation?

ADORNO. . . . Indeed: it no longer has anything to do with it. To a large extent it's turning into a *show*. And the line between what's designated by the term *show business* nowadays,[6] between that business and official musical culture, has long since become ideological, a total sham. In reality there's scarcely any sort of difference between these spheres any more. These things also result in the complete distortion of a conductor's actual achievement. His task consists in nothing less than getting to know a work down to its smallest objective details, in attaining complete analytic mastery of it, in developing a precise conception of it and then in conveying and actualizing this conception as rationally as possible. What's being produced now in lieu of this, thanks to these televisual machinations, is the illusion that the conductor is a kind of magician, a medicine man, who through the pure exertion of his will or some other refractory force is making something happen that can probably only ever happen as a result of thoughtful and painstaking rehearsals. In a certain sense this modus operandi does an injustice to a musician of Karajan's stature and quality, because it accentuates certain features that whatever else they may be are quite unrepresentative of his best qualities.

SPIEGEL. But isn't Herbert von Karajan himself one of the main proponents of this televised music? We recall his famous statement: 'What good does it do me when 6,000 people in Salzburg hear me? The whole world should be in the audience.' He's already thinking about worldwide satellite telecasts, and he even believes that television is the quintessential future medium of music.

---

6 *Show* and *show business* are in English in the original. [Trans.]

ADORNO. Nowadays there's a kind of secondary naivety among artists; not just the primary sort of naivety, the unjustly much-praised cult of primordial nature, but rather a kind of naivety that suggests to the artist that the reified, commodified mode of activity he's locked into is something God-given, something absolute. It's the naivety of someone who without thinking too much about it is kowtowing to the fiats of the culture industry. This naivety causes them to utter pronouncements like the one by Mr von Karajan that you just quoted. Here I think it would quite simply be helpful for someone to make a point of drawing such artists' attention to the problems we've been discussing here.

SPIEGEL. Professor Adorno, a pedagogical argument is also always trotted out in connection with this. According to this argument, televised music gives consumers a preliminary introduction to the work and thereby stimulates them to attend concerts or opera performances in person. What do you think of this kind of musical therapy?

ADORNO. It's wrong. I don't think there's any such thing as a pedagogical path to the essential that starts out by getting people to concentrate on the inessential. This sort of attention that fixates on the inessential actually indurates; it becomes habitual and thereby interferes with one's experience of the essential. I don't believe that when it comes to art there can ever be any processes of gradual familiarization that gradually lead from what's wrong to what's right. Artistic experience always consists in qualitative leaps and never in that murky sort of process.

SPIEGEL. Don't you also think it's possible that over time the presentation of the same thing over and over again on television will actually cause the charm to wear off and that the intended pedagogical goal of awakening interest will be turned into its exact opposite—namely, disgust with these things?

ADORNO. That sounds plausible. But of course psychologically speaking we're largely dealing here with an infantile, meaning a regressive, mechanism—the child that keeps insisting on having the same food—and so unfortunately I have so far encountered very little of this disgust and this surfeiting and much more of a diminution of the capacity for artistic experience, meaning any sort of possibility of leaving oneself open to anything that's qualitatively new and different. I would almost say that these procedures are more likely augmenting people's aversion to the new, to things that aren't pre-categorized. In any case, in the so-called cultural domain I can so far discern no symptoms of what in America they call sales resistance,[7] meaning resistance to the presentation of the same commodities over and over again.

SPIEGEL. But won't television be required to take on new responsibilities once the provincial opera houses and orchestras all but stop receiving government subsidies, as is of course very likely to happen in the course of the next few decades?

ADORNO. If, say, the broadcasters were subsequently to provide increasingly substantial support to the indigenous orchestras in the German provinces, orchestras that have of course always

---

7 *Sales resistance* is in English in the original. [Trans.]

figured among the greatest assets of German musical life and whose collapse would be a terrible loss, that would be a very good thing. As far as opera goes, I think it will perhaps survive this century and will hardly survive the next one. I can easily envisage a culture in which opera has disappeared in a way similar to that in which a whole array of other art forms have— for example, realistic portraiture in painting. After that, people who take a specialized interest in it will just listen to it on records. I've honestly got to say it would be better to have no opera at all than the transmogrification of every conceivable opera into yet another *Der Rosenkavalier*. Recently Pierre Boulez has quite rightly highlighted the crisis in opera. I fully concur with his opinion of the problematic nature of opera as an art form traditionally manifested in association with the great opera houses. What's going through an acute crisis is opera itself as an art form, not the public's interest in it, because they're still running in droves to performances of *Aida* and *Die Meistersinger*. But the composition of operas in the traditional sense—even in the sense of *Wozzeck* and *Lulu* and *Moses and Aron*—is over and done with.

SPIEGEL. There's yet another argument with which the cultural-industrialists rally to televised music's defence. The fact that operas and concerts are reaching a mass audience via the television screen is something they equate with a cultural resurgence. What do you think of that?

ADORNO. Once again I regard this as a completely wrong argument. Although I have no desire to put in even the faintest of good words for some fusty ideal of interiority, it seems to me that above all something profoundly inauthentic is going on here, because the works themselves aren't indifferent to the manner in which they are presented. A televised *Figaro* is no longer *Figaro*. Consequently, when the masses come into contact with it, they are no longer by any means coming into contact with the thing itself but rather with a pre-dissected, cliche-ridden product of the culture industry, which gives them the illusory sense that they could become actively involved in culture. For quite some time now, so-called great, traditional music has been following the same trajectory as the one completed by Raphael's Madonna della Sedia once it was hanging on the wall of each and every petit-bourgeois bedroom.

SPIEGEL. So then, Professor Adorno, are you really of the opinion that for the time being televised music is a pointless rigmarole?

ADORNO. Indeed, I really am of that opinion. Televised concerts and televised operas are a complete waste of cultural activity.

SPIEGEL. Professor Adorno, we thank you for this interview.

ORPHEUS IN THE UNDERWORLD

ON CHART-TOPPING GRAMOPHONE RECORDS

AND THE GERMAN RECORD-BUYING PUBLIC

It would be naive to attempt to contemplate the sales chart for so-called serious music simply as a gauge of public taste. The public's preferences have been shaped by too many factors to be taken at face value. Its politics of selection are driven by the centrally governing authorities. Only what the record companies include in their production schedule and release with auspicious prospects of distribution on a massive scale can become a chart-topper. This might be the main reason for the cheapness of almost all the records on the chart; on the other hand this cheapness is presumably also dependent on the pre-accumulated success of individual records, which are then thrown into the marketplace with budget price-tags, much like paperbacks. Advertising contributes as well—not only via explicit commendation, but sometimes even in the very titles of the discs, e.g. *Concert for Millions*; it extends into the attractive force of visibility, of catch-phrases, of the prestige of individual works and, above all, of famous performers. All of this likewise exerts an influence on the public's reactions, just as conversely these

---

* 'Orpheus in der Unterwelt' (1968) in *Gesammelte Schriften*, 'Band 19: Musikalische Schriften VI'.

Originally published in *Der Spiegel* (11 November 1968), pp. 200–206.

factors have been multifariously generated by the ossification of the standards of public taste over several decades. If one speaks critically of manipulation, this is not to be regarded as referring to a unilateral duty levied from on high. The already-engrained status quo is tenaciously reverenced and reproduced. Only the most refined investigations could separate what has been foisted on the public from what lurks within it, to the extent that such a distinction still has any meaning. The practical sociology of music has hitherto completely ignored such questions and gainsaid them out of the world wherever possible via its own definition of them.

Having conceded all of this from the outset, one can most certainly have recourse to the sales-chart as an inventory of dominant and dominated musical taste and try to discern what it perchance divulges. Only interested parties will misunderstand this analysis as an aspersion on the public and turn what it discovers about the true state of affairs into an accusation against the analyst. Admittedly, such blame-shifting via the imputation of intellectual snobbery is quite common nowadays. Contempt for the masses is the charge invariably levelled at anyone who articulates what the world has done to the masses and what is reflected back by them and who does not bow down before the outrage that the consciousness of human beings has been condemned to suffer and that they cling to in a fashion that Kant would have termed self-imposed.[1] Ideologues, who pay the loudest lip-service to values, are in the cynical habit of commending values to demographic groups that have invariably been brought into being and kept in line by the powers that be. These ideologues are the true snobs: contempt for human beings

---

1 An allusion to the opening sentence of Kant's essay 'Beantwortung der Frage: Was ist Aufklärung?' [An Answer to the Question: What is Enlightenment?]: 'Enlightenment is man's emergence from his self-imposed tutelage.' [Trans.]

fairly oozes from their indulgent slogan 'Just let the people have their fun.' The feasible emancipation of humanity is anathema in their eyes; by now, the fact that this emancipation has not yet been achieved is entirely the fault of cliques with a controlling interest in preventing it.

One must not shrink from asking the question of whether the choice made by consumers is specific at all, of whether it is even based on what they have heard and experienced in relation to music. The surprisingly high demands made by some works, the utter inanity of others, render this improbable. For some consumers it may be more important to reaffirm their own status by buying a disc than to treat themselves to what they actually like. This is complemented by such obstacles to making a good selection as the notorious ban on packages of trial discs.

Not to put too fine a point on it, the most conspicuous thing about the chart is everything that is *missing* from it—first and foremost, the entire modern repertoire, including middle-of-the-road and well-established works that happen to have been written after 1900, like *Der Rosenkavalier*. This aversion to modernity is taken for granted, even though music that hails from the same intellectual environment as that of its presumptive listeners should actually be more highly cherished by them. But they favour compositions whose content lags behind their own experience, sometimes so far behind as to lead them to believe that this content is an ideal beyond their reach rather than something readily accessible to them in real life. Then there is a threshold of complexity: nothing that is as richly and densely wrought as Brahms, and that therefore requires as much concentration, appears on the chart; nor does any Wagner.

The last three Mozart symphonies and all of Schubert and Schumann are notably absent from the chart's roster of works of the so-called classical and Romantic periods. But especially glaring is the absence of the entire corpus of great chamber music from Haydn to Schoenberg.

There can be no doubt that this corpus as a whole—and not just the late Beethoven quartets—is on par with, and in many ways superior to, the symphonic repertoire. But the bourgeois worship of lavish means in isolation from their ends has obviously taken possession of musical taste, especially among those new groups of listeners who are unfamiliar with the intimate musical tradition and who first come into contact with serious music via the techno-logical media. They are smitten with *glamour*—this English word defies translation—whose template is supplied by tunes from com-mercial films. Pomp and splendour take precedence over internal structure, over what is going on inside the piece as a composition in the fullest sense. A primitive concept of variegation seems to be exerting a veritably hypnotic force, as if people believed that in purchasing a record they were being issued a voucher for the delivery of a smattering of colour to their lives.

On taking in the entire chart at a glance, one is initially struck by the medley-like character of the many of the discs in virtue of their inclusion of a multitude of things in one place. Relatively short and undemanding pieces are strung together on each disc; these pieces exact little concentration and do not expect the listener to attend at all closely to the development of a formal argument. A crude diversity of offerings blends smoothly into the listener's dis-tracted consciousness. The old-style café music is dying out; the word *medley* is now given a wide berth by the sales charts for serious music, but they are the shamefaced heirs of that déclassé branch of the musical family.

Even though the chart claims to be dealing exclusively with serious music, many of the discs at the top of it are simply highbrow entertainment, representatives of a category to which the Americans without a trace of irony apply the invincible label *semi-classical*. They bear witness to an ideological compromise. On the one hand nobody wants to sacrifice his cultural pretensions; the aficionados of highbrow entertainment must be allowed to fancy themselves intellectually and socially superior to those of light-music, the hit parade, and, most recently, pop. On the other hand, the repertoire of the semi-classical is as complaisantly easy on the listeners' ears as light music. They can revel in its readily understood melodies in the upper voices, its highly simple rhythmic schemata, its insinuated emotional gestures. The customary administrative division between serious and light is actualized ad absurdum. Many of the chart-toppers that are classified as serious according to accepted standards are intrinsically light in character or at any rate rendered banal and shop-worn by countless repetitions: what was serious can become light. Moreover, performance practice as perpetuated by the chart-toppers frequently strives for an accommodation of seriousness to lightness. The reification of the cleanly divided musical domains collects its debt in full. Whatever is opposed to such reification has already been overtaken by it in virtue of the division.

The Wunderlich disc and the *Concert for Millions* that figure at third and fourth places on the chart are light music in disguise. Wunderlich starts out with two Mozart arias as with an obligatory examination passed with flying colours only to move onto the most famous operatic showpieces like 'Ach wie so trügerisch'[2] and Puccini

---

2 'Ach wie so trügerisch' [Oh, How Deceitful], the standard German translation of 'La donna è mobile' from Verdi's *Rigoletto*. [Trans.]

followed by Lehár and finally end with a few unspeakable pieces of rubbish; whether they are supposed to be the 'folksongs' promised on the jacket remains undetermined. The late singer's lack of disdain for kitsch is milked as a praiseworthy quality by the scribbler responsible for the liner notes: 'It was completely in keeping with his outlook on life to sing folksongs and bravura arias from operettas. He gave his all to beauty.' As if the difference between the beautiful and the hideous were not precisely the difference between Mozart and Messrs Grossmann and Neuendorff;[3] with such pieces dirigiste cultural semi-literacy is directly furthering barbarism. Wunderlich displays his magnificent voice with great cultivation, a fair amount of monotony and little contrast; it has obviously been boosted by the sound engineer.

The *Concert for Millions* by contrast consists of nothing but cultural treasures, several of them excellently performed—for example, the 'Hallelujah' Chorus from the *Messiah* and the overture to *The Magic Flute* under Böhm's baton and the scherzo from the incidental music to *A Midsummer Night's Dream* under Kubelik's; others, like the first movement of the 'Moonlight' Sonata, played much too slowly, with preposterously melodized triplets, are less easy to stomach. At the end Karajan officiates at a performance of the Radetzky March; he first steps into action much earlier with

---

3 *Grossmann*: Paul Grossman, the author of the lyrics of the song 'Zwei dunkle Augen' [Two Dark Eyes], the penultimate cut on the posthumous Fritz Wunderlich LP *Der grosse lyrishce Tenor* (the composer of the music of 'Zwei dunkle Augen' being Carl Heins); *Neuendorff*: Adolf Neuendorff, the German-born American composer of *The Rat-Charmer of Hamelin*, an operetta containing the aria 'Wandern, ach wandern' [Wandering, Ah, Wandering], the final cut on the Wunderlich LP. [Trans.]

the famous air from Bach's D major suite;[4] unsurpassable in sonority, unaffectedly ingratiating, but melodically somewhat shapeless, such that the inconceivably grandiose melodic line, whose lustre no amount of wear and tear could ever scuff or tarnish, fails to come fully into its own. All told, the record suggests that one may cheaply have the entirety of musical culture delivered to one's home in a single densely packed bundle of top-class performances, and that one could comfortably assimilate this entirety in less than an hour.

In starkest contrast to these stands the group of records doing business as Baroque Music. Two such discs, the first of which is dedicated to Handel, are situated at the top of the chart; they are sequestered from a third one entitled *Virtuoso Trumpet Concertos*. Most likely in the eyes of these records' purchasers the concept of the baroque really only functions as a guarantor of prestige; it is impossible to imagine that all of this stuff, much of it quite lethally boring, could both captivate the most musical and entertain the least musical of listeners. The title *Festive Baroque* that has been found for the second-place finisher provides part of the explanation for these discs' success. Another part is doubtless to be found in an intoxicating feeling of edification devoid of any regard for the underlying musical architecture, together with the usual adulation of stylishness. In the case of the Handel discs the nicknames 'Fireworks Music' and 'Water Music' also come into play by fraudulently promising a version of impressionism, for these works assuredly contain no *reflets sur l'eau* or *feu d'artifice*. Despite everything, this group is comparable to elevated entertainment in its effortless admissibility

---

4 *The famous air from Bach's D major suite*: 'Air on the G String', August Wilhelmj's arrangement of the second movement of Bach's Orchestral Suite No. 3 in D major, BWV 1068. [Trans.]

into the latter's watertight pigeonholes. The fact remains that Handel's superiority to the rest of the chirpers is quite palpable: amid all the ephemerality of the routine, he was a composer of great power and magnanimity. Admittedly the range of the basic figures available to him is so limited that even here monotony quickly sets in and leaves listeners with little consolation apart from the knowledge that at least they already know what is going to happen next. Mozart, who in Schoenberg's words cut metres and metres of sequences from the *Messiah*, was in the right as a composer, whatever may be said against his arrangements from the point of view of the history of style. Handel's synthesis of Italian operatic homophony and German counterpoint—a synthesis officially accredited to him by the historians of music—can only sound convincing to somebody who doesn't know what counterpoint is: Handel fails to honour the obligations that are imposed on the composer from the start of every polyphonic composition. No fabric of voices is ever fully woven; the nexus of voices never establishes the form; in their brittleness and illogicality, the expositions of his fugues tend to founder in harmonic shoals as soon as the development starts. In performances his stiff inner accents fall all at once on notes tied across the bar line.

The disc entitled *Festive Baroque* presents Mouret's relatively variety-packed and merry 'Fanfares', Handel's admittedly feeble and flaccid 100th Psalm, and a concerto for two horns by Telemann, a work lacking any kind of physiognomy but also no worse than most others of this sort. Bach's Second Brandenburg Concerto, the one with the high trumpet, has somehow stumbled onto this record. This work's superiority to the rest is awe-inspiringly obvious, but in such company even Bach gets sucked into the maelstrom of mindless

211

tootling. What comes to the fore here is the sort of typicality that wrongly awakens a sense of the compulsory and authentic in guileless souls. Here Bach was manifestly obliged to try to accept as a stylistic imperative that infelicitous custom of having the leading concertante motifs bite each other's tails. For all its fame this concerto does not display the real Bach; rather, it is an example of what is nowadays known as a contribution—a contribution to the golden surplus of superfluity.

Regarding the disc of trumpet music,[5] it may at least be said to its credit that in defiance of what one might have feared from this chart-topping instrument it does not pander to military desiderata; the pieces on it are of a pre-Frederician innocence and possibly potentiate nothing but tedium. What a strange emotional constitution the Bishop of Olmütz must have had if he expected to be entertained by these sorts of short-winded compositions that hardly ever break free of the principal scale degrees and resemble one another as closely as rotten eggs. This disc comprises works by his favourite composers, a few of whom, such as Biber and Poglietti, were quite famous in their day. May they rest in peace, the peace of archives and dissertations. The masterly trumpeter Scherbaum deserves better vehicles.

In the third group, the Slavic complex, at least something is happening. They provide fodder to the emotional listener, who pic-

---

5 Although the disc at No. 10 in *Der Spiegel*'s chart is *Virtuose Trompetenkonzerte III* (Deutsche Grammophon 136 518 SLPEM), Adorno appears to be referencing a different LP featuring Adolf Scherbaum as trumpet soloist, *Virtuose Trompetenmusik aus Böhmen* (Deutsche Grammophon 136 549 SLPEM), whose liner notes present it as a collection of works 'composed for the musical establishment of Prince-Bishop Karl Liechtenstein of Olmütz', including concertos by Heinrich Ignaz Franz Biber and Alessandro Poglietti. [Trans.]

tures Slavs as savages oscillating dramatically between melancholy sentimentality and Sarmatian violence. In sixth place the disc called *Music from the Great Tradition*, an *Introduction to the World of Slavic Music*, succeeds thanks to performances recorded in Prague. It scarcely effects such an introduction via Borodin's *Steppes of Central Asia*, a piece that has long since sunk into the sphere of spa music, and an ultra-academic product like the *Capriccio espagnol* of Rimsky-Korsakov, to whom nothing better occurs than the dreary jumping-about of the kind of ballet that prides itself on its classicality. A fragment of Janáček's *Glagolithic Mass* doesn't help here either.

But then there's Tchaikovsky—the victors in the Russian competition named after him and a disc by Karajan with the Berlin Philharmonic. Here the public probably cast its sincere vote. In Germany, Tchaikovsky has a hard time being taken seriously as a great composer. By now he has manifestly gotten quite popular in defiance of the cultural tradition and has come to occupy the place in consumers' hearts that he has long held in America. However tirelessly virtuoso conductors may have always given him their all, audiences are now spontaneously embracing him. His giftedness is patently audible; genius and mediocrity are commingled in the most curious fashion. His facility at devising figures that are extraordinarily powerful, and for that very reason often frankly vulgar, is impressive. But the solution to the mystery of the effect is to be found in a very deep stratum of infantilism. Tchaikovsky's music, that of a man condemned to unhappiness by Victorian prudery, is nourished by an ungovernable longing for happiness; it gets drunk on the fulfilment that is denied to him, a man who regales himself with grand passion in his daydreams. This is the way children orient themselves towards happiness; the greatest artists are granted the privilege of holding onto some portion of this orientation into adulthood. But this is only possible in a fragmentary way, in the recollection of what is irrecoverably lost, in the yearning for what can never again be equalled. Tchaikovsky's longing for happiness has not experienced this fragmentation in musical terms: his pictorial world is not sublimated but crassly left intact. This is as emphatically responsible for the striking extremity of his themes as for their ultra-distinctiveness and immediacy. For all the dexterousness of his symphonism, it is hardly symphonic: it is utterly devoid of any capacity for integration. It paves the way for atomistic listening. A short path leads from string-section themes like the ones from *Romeo and Juliet* and the Piano Concerto to Gershwin via Rachmaninoff:[6] they are prototypes of hit tunes in whose company one can supposedly count on feeling that one is a person of rank despite their popularity. Whether his success is also being abetted by repressed Slavophilia, an anti-Western element of the German mindset subsisting beneath the official Russophobia, is difficult to determine; this element has so many things going for it. That Karajan's interpretation of *Romeo and Juliet* does its unsurpassable utmost to wring out every drop of effect contained in this piece, probably Tchaikovsky's most powerful work, goes without saying. The winners of the competition, Tretyakov and especially the boy pianist Sokolov, will disappoint nobody. Chart-toppers must meet certain standards; the goods are exchanged in kind.

Now for the pièce de résistance, the Beethoven discs, at fifth and ninth places on the chart. Artur Rubinstein has recorded the

---

6 *The Piano Concerto*: as before, presumably the Piano Concerto No. 1 in B-flat minor, op. 23. [Trans.]

complete piano concertos supplely, articulately, and unlike many pianists of the following generation he does not give one the feeling that he is actually handling Beethoven like jazz. The audience is soft-soaped by such propensities of his as the slight over-extension of lyrical themes; in contravention of the indication of andante con moto, the tempo of the slow movement of the G major concerto is sluggish. The foundational rhythm of the principal theme of the rondo finale of the E-flat major concerto,[7] a rhythm of decisive significance for the entire movement, is not hewn out of the surrounding material with sufficiently sculptural plasticity. But the success of these discs is justified, and even understandable from a musician's point of view. Not, to be sure, that the colossal passage for the double basses at the end of the Andante of the G major concerto is patently mistaken for accompaniment by the master engineer—oh, what masters!—and kept inaudible.

The choice of the *Missa Solemnis* under Karajan's baton with the Vienna Choral Society and, once again, the Berlin Philharmonic, is quite surprising. The work is unfathomable, and to this day it has yet to be fully deciphered by anybody. In its outward aspect it is anything but intelligible; the listeners allow themselves to be convinced by the master that it is his oeuvre plus accompli without being able to maintain without scruple that they can fathom its quality with their ears alone; a textbook example of what may be termed mandatory listening. All the same, it is hardly by chance that this disc has found favour with this phenomenon. Karajan disguises its enigmatic character via euphony, with the aid of the finest

---

7 *The G major concerto*: No. 4, op. 58; *the E-flat major concerto*: No. 5, op. 73, the 'Emperor'. [Trans.]

available vocal soloists—Gundula Janowitz, Christa Ludwig, Fritz Wunderlich and Walter Berry. Keeping the sonic mirror polished outweighs all other concerns; thus the central piece, the fugue *Et vitam venturi* from the Credo, is handled with indescribable circumspection and moderation, so that absolutely nothing happens; this at the cost of its intensity. The instrumental basses are banished into the background to no advantage of the harmonic process. Amid all the mastery, the primacy of the sonority blurs contours and phrasing. On the other hand it is probably the engineer who is to blame for the fact that the beginning of the *Et carnatus est* is virtually inaudible at a normal volume setting. It is nevertheless astonishing that Karajan, who enjoys the reputation of also taking great pains about the details of technical reproduction, highlights passages that are irreconcilable with the ideal of sonic continuity that he usually evinces in his practice. A suggestion is not amiss here— namely, that on every record player, the volume-control dial should be equipped with a scale—in each case one commensurate with the apparatus in question—indicating decibel levels. Then the decibel levels intended by the conductors—who, like the directors of films, bear ultimate responsibility for the whole—would be required to be noted on all records. That would constitute something like a translation of the governing principle of the metronome into the terms of dynamics. It would guarantee a certain measure of objectivity in the ratios of sonic forces during the playing of the disc.

Not a few readers will truculently demur, 'What difference does it make, as long as people are entertained by all this?' But the very concept of entertainment is of disputable validity. It remains true that in a state of affairs in which technology is supposedly making human beings' lives easier, people ubiquitously feel overwhelmed and are seeking compensation for the repugnant labour that, now as before, is imposed on them by the relations of production, and that this sought-after compensation merely covertly replicates that labour's monotony. To do battle against the right to entertainment and force culture down the throats of an unwilling populace would be schoolmasterly presumption. Nevertheless, entertainment objectively does that populace an objective injustice; entertainment is imposed on them, and they subjectively crave it. It is nothing other than a substitute for what is denied human beings elsewhere, and this is demonstrated by the subaltern, spurious and friable quality of most of the material that only showcases culture for entertainment's sake while at the same time repressing and ridiculing it. Via their transformation into commodities, cultural treasures are having the life driven out of them. Jazz fans have sound instincts to the extent that they give pride of place to the spontaneity of the performance and of their own reaction to it, even if their object of adulation is admittedly no less of a commodity than the musical culture industry against which they rebel. What is happening in this industry attests to the emergence of something far-reaching, the miscarriage of culture among those who fancy they possess it and for that very reason do not possess it. From time to time, one asks oneself what is still left to be defended against the onslaught of open and admitted barbarism. The world of entertainment [*Unterhaltung*] is the underworld [*Unterwelt*] that passes itself off as Heaven.

1968

Translator's Acknowledgement

The translator wishes to extend his sincerest thanks to flowerville for her invaluable insight and assistance in reviewing the complete preliminary draft of the translation.